A Ministry of Consolation

Involving Your Parish in the *Order of Christian Funerals*

Mary Alice Piil, C.S.J.
Joseph DeGrocco
Rose Mary Cover

A Liturgical Press Book

THE LITURGICAL PRESS
Collegeville, Minnesota

Cover design by Ann Blattner

1   2   3   4   5   6   7   8

Library of Congress Cataloging-in-Publication Data

Cover, Rose Mary, 1943–
    A ministry of consolation : involving your parish in the Order of
Christian funerals / Rose Mary Cover, Joseph DeGrocco, Mary Alice
Piil.
        p.   cm.
    ISBN 0-8146-2460-X
    1. Catholic Church.   Order of Christian funerals.   2. Funeral
service—Catholic Church.   3. Bereavement—Religious aspects—
Catholic Church.   4. Lay ministry—Catholic Church.   I. DeGrocco,
Joseph, 1961– .   II. Piil, Mary Alice, 1943– .   III. Title.
BX2035.6.F8523C68   1997
264'.020985—dc21
                                                                                96-36774
                                                                                CIP

To Bishop John R. McGann, D.D.,
on the twenty-fifth anniversary of his ordination to the episcopacy
and twentieth anniversary as bishop of the Diocese of Rockville Centre,
in grateful appreciation for his leadership and vision
in promoting and supporting so many varied ministries
in our local church.
June 1996

Contents

Introduction

You and your family have experienced the loss of your seventy-three-year-old mother. You arrive at the church to celebrate her funeral Mass. The funeral director ushers you into the church and lines everyone up behind the coffin. You notice that a priest is standing in the center aisle in front of the coffin. He begins the Mass with the blessing of the coffin, even though the people behind you cannot really see or hear what's going on. The pall bearers hired by the funeral home—men you have never seen before—place the white pall over the coffin. You notice that it's crooked and one of the corners is askew, but there is no time for you to even straighten it out as the procession immediately then moves forward. The entrance song is being sung, and when you get to your seat you try to find it in the music book, but before you are successful in doing so, the song ends. The priest does the readings himself, and you think to yourself that Mom would have liked a particular Scripture reading other than the one he chose. The priest's homily is hope-filled but somewhat generic—speaking of the promise of the resurrection but not really making any connections with your mother's life, a life that you feel was a tremendous witness to Christian faith.

You can't help gasping when you hear the offertory song; Mom always hated that one! You glance over your shoulder during the Eucharistic Prayer and feel a little sorry for your brothers and sisters. They have not been to Mass for a long time and are a little lost as to what to do; they feel out of place at a time when feeling comfortable would help the healing process. You wish that someone would direct and help them; you wish you had the nerve to do it, but somehow it would seem out-of-place. On the way out of church, the priest shakes everyone's hand and sincerely offers his condolences. You thank him for his wishes, but can't help feeling that a certain "assembly line" atmosphere pervaded the entire ritual. Your mother was a member of the parish for fifty years, and you've been a member all your life; while everything about the Mass was proper, you can't shake the feeling that your mother and all of you in the family deserved something a little more warm and personal.

You and your family have experienced the loss of your seventy-three-year-old mother. You arrive at the church to celebrate her funeral Mass. As you get out of the car and walk to the church entrance, a member of the parish who has been a companion to you since your mother's death and who led the vigil prayer service the night before greets you. The companion greets you with a smile and greets your brothers, sisters, and aunts and uncles by name. Your relatives from another parish are surprised that anyone even knows who they are! The companion introduces you to the priest who will be presiding at Mass, and the priest takes the time to shake hands with all in the immediate family, expressing his condolences to them by name. Those who will be in the procession behind the coffin and those already seated in the church receive a booklet specially prepared for this liturgy. The booklet contains your mother's name and the choices of readings and hymns your family has selected with the assistance of the companion. People from the parish wearing name tags identifying them as "ministers of consolation" help everyone gather behind the coffin so that they can see and be a part of the Introductory Rites. You and your brothers and sisters lovingly drape your mother's coffin with the white funeral pall. Each of you tenderly makes sure that the pall drapes properly and is smooth so that it gives proper dignity to her body.

As the readings are proclaimed, you listen to the words of the Scriptures as you never have before. They are familiar readings, and you have heard them often, yet somehow this time they are different. This occasion has given to them a depth, and a smile comes to your face as you recall the reasons you and your brothers and sisters chose each of the readings. What the priest says in the homily is pleasantly surprising; you find it very comforting to hear how he puts together details of your mother's life and elements of the Christian understanding of death. It's almost as though the priest and your mother were friends!

You're so proud as two of the grandchildren bring forward the gifts of bread and wine. They do this without a hitch, thanks to the guidance of the companion, who is right there with the family helping them through the Mass. You happen to look around and you notice people there who are from the parish even though they did not know your mother all that well. You get a sudden feeling that your mother, indeed all of you, really belong to this parish family if these people care enough to be here at this time.

As you sing the Communion song, you remember that it was one of Mom's favorites. When the Mass is over and you all leave the church, the priest, your companion, and other people from the parish again offer their condolences and support. Later in the day, after the cemetery service, when you are all relaxing and having a meal at your house, your brothers and sisters comment on the warmth and love that was evident in the church; they remark that Mom was treated as a very special person in that parish. One brother, who has not been to church in fifteen years, is particularly moved, and comments that this is how he thought church always should be—people caring about people. One of the reasons he stopped going to Mass was that he felt the Catholic Church was too big and impersonal. But today meant so much to him! With tears in his eyes, he mentions that he just might even start going to Mass again on Sundays.

Think about the last funeral you attended. Which of the above descriptions comes closer to your experience? What was your experience as a member of that praying community? Did you feel welcomed? Did you feel your presence truly made a difference? Was it obvious that those in attendance were an important part of the ritual? Was there the sense that the deceased for whom everyone was praying was a unique individual whose gifts and presence to the parish community meant something? Did you have the sense that together everyone was entering into the mystery of what we believe about death leading to new life in Christ?

Unfortunately, the experience of many people when they attend funeral Masses is closer to the first scenario than it is to the second. This probably does not result from any deliberate intention but rather just from a sense that if the priest knows how to say the Mass and the music director knows how to pick music, what else is needed? This overlooks, however, the tremendous potential inherent in the ritual itself to touch people in a very personal way and to bring alive the role of the larger community in the funeral rites.

In the Ministry of Consolation, parishioners become involved in ministry at the time of the wake service and funeral Mass. It has primarily a liturgical focus, and is not meant to be a bereavement outreach or grief counseling. These are later steps and an important follow-up, but not covered under the auspices of this ministry. The Ministry of Consolation provides personal contact, warmth, and outreach to people at a time when it is very necessary. It is primary evangelization.

This book outlines a method of establishing a Ministry of Consolation in your parish that will help you celebrate funeral liturgies which leave people with the experience described in the second scenario.* This ministry is a marvelous tool for evangelization and outreach, since it touches people at critical moments in their lives and presents to them an image of church that is caring, concerned, and personal. A Ministry of Consolation can revitalize and renew parishes that have grown lukewarm, and it can bring even more life to those already alive. It will touch and transform not only those who are mourning the loss of a loved one but also all those involved in the ministry. Again and again those who have experienced a funeral Mass enhanced by the Ministry of Consolation talk about what a wonderful experience of Church it is and how comforting the celebration becomes.

This book examines the *Order of Christian Funerals* from the perspective of a Ministry of Consolation so that a parish can establish this ministry. We will deal primarily with the funeral Mass itself, making applications and suggestions for that liturgy *vis-à-vis* the Ministry of Consolation. Once the basic format is in place for the funeral Mass, your parish may apply and extend the same principles to the various other rites (e.g., vigil service, gatherings in the presence of the body, etc.).

Chapter 1 looks at the theology and mystery of Christian death and discusses a renewed understanding of Church based on what the *Rite of Christian Initiation of Adults* has taught us about the role of the community. Chapter 2 describes the rite of the funeral Mass in the *Order of Christian Funerals* from the perspective of the people who would be involved in a Ministry of Consolation. Chapter 3 considers specific adaptations that parishes may want to be aware of. In the margins in these chapters are reflections of a companion. Chapter 4 outlines five training sessions. The appendix provides sample materials that a parish can use in implementing a Ministry of Consolation. Throughout it all, our goal is to provide the opportunity for the celebration of the funeral rites in all their depth and beauty, allowing the consoling power of the risen Christ to come forth in our communal prayer and participation.

---

*The Ministry of Consolation as described in this book is an outgrowth of a doctoral project done by Rev. Ed Maurer in fulfillment of his doctor of ministry degree at the Seminary of the Immaculate Conception, Huntington, New York. The title of the project was *Lay Ministries in the Order of Christian Funerals*.

1 The Theology and Mystery of Christian Death

Every culture, every religious tradition, has some story and ritual associated with the death of one of its members. These rituals often focus on the absence of the deceased or on the grief of the mourners. Some speak of an afterlife for the deceased while others point to a possible union of the living and the dead at some future moment. The Christian community too has rituals to bring to closure the physical life of one of its members and to console those who remain. Unique to the Christian experience of death however is the gift of Jesus Christ who in his death on the cross taught us how to die and in his resurrection opened for us the possibility of new life. Christ's paschal mystery, his entry into death and resurrection, provides the Christian with the model of dying and rising to new life.

One of the greatest contributions of the liturgical reform of the twentieth century was the renewed emphasis on the paschal mystery, the dying and rising of Jesus Christ. This caused the Church to rethink the funeral liturgy as it had been celebrated according to the Tridentine Rite. Many will recall the emphasis placed on death as the end, the day of wrath. Little if any attention was given to the fact that Christ's death led to resurrection and that the Christian who entered into the mystery with Christ in baptism was called to the fullness of life received in him. Thus the Church is able to state in the General Introduction to the *Order of Christian Funerals:*

> In the face of death, the Church confidently proclaims that God has created each person for eternal life and that Jesus, the Son of God, by his death and resurrection, has broken the chains of sin and death that bound humanity. Christ "achieved his task of redeeming humanity and giving perfect glory to God, principally by the paschal mystery of his blessed passion, resurrection from the dead, and glorious ascension" (*OCF* #1).

The symbolism of the *Order of Christian Funerals* frequently reminds us of baptism, for our initiation began our participation in the mystery of Christ's death and resurrection that would culminate in our death. "Dying you destroyed our death, rising you restored our life, Lord Jesus come in glory" are words on our lips as we participate in the Eucharistic Prayer at Mass. Daily we rehearse that final participation in Christ's mystery by dying the various deaths of life. By embracing these deaths as Christ embraced his, we learn how to die. We prepare for the ultimate and final death that will lead to our final movement from death to new life, the life of the saints in glory.

During life Christ calls the Christian to union in a most personal relationship, a relationship fulfilled at the moment of death when one encounters Christ face to face. At this moment the goal of the life of the Christian is achieved when the individual, faithful in life to Christ, now enters into total union with him.

The *Order of Christian Funerals* speaks clearly of the fact that the Christian is never alone in this daily journey of life and death. Both prayers and readings found in the rite echo the message of the Second Vatican Council that says, "It was from the side of Christ as he slept the sleep of death upon the cross that there came forth 'the wondrous sacrament of the whole Church'" (*Sacrosanctum concilium* #5*). Christ did not leave the individual alone but rather left the Church to be his presence in the world, to be his support for each individual disciple living a life in faith.

As believers then, we live the mystery of Christ's dying and rising, but we live it in union with our brothers and sisters who in union with Christ share that most intimate of communions in the Spirit with each and all. In the thirty years since the Second Vatican Council, the entire membership of the Church has renewed its understanding of how each member participates. The Constitution on the Church challenged all the faithful to full participation in the work of bringing the Gospel to all people. Each member of the Church has the responsibility of building up the body according to the specific talents of the person. But each one must do something to foster greater participation of all in the mission of Christ. This challenge is brought out clearly in the *Rite of Christian Initiation of Adults*. Here we see that all support the spiritual journey of each individual to full participation in the paschal mystery. The task of assisting individual members in their faith development is not given to the clergy alone. Christ calls other individuals within the community who have the potential to assist the development of faith, be they parents, teachers, or other significant lay members of the community, to share their faith so that the faith of others might increase. This lay min-

---

*Austin Flannery, ed., *Vatican Council II: The Conciliar and Post Conciliar Documents* (Dublin: Dominican Publications, 1992) 3.

Church with me

When I met the family at the funeral home that first afternoon, I prayed with them using the rite, "Gathering in the Presence of the Body." The next morning, we met to plan the funeral liturgy. When sickness and scheduling problems prevented the presence of a priest at the vigil service, a lector from the couple's "regular" Mass agreed to accompany me to lead the prayer.

On her way out of church the next morning, the widow told the presider, "My church was with me all the way." And so it was.

istry might call for specific involvement in the faith life of another or it might take the stance of prayer on the part of some for others. Whatever the role, each member is asked to participate according to individual potentials.

This understanding of church is the basis of the *Order of Christian Funerals:*

> At the death of a Christian, whose life of faith was begun in the waters of baptism and strengthened at the eucharistic table, the Church intercedes on behalf of the deceased because of its confident belief that death is not the end nor does it break the bonds forged in life. The Church also ministers to the sorrowing and consoles them in the funeral rites with the comforting word of God and the sacrament of the Eucharist (*OCF* #4).

The first role of the Church—both the universal and the local community—is to offer prayer for the deceased. In this prayer of intercession the Church both "commends the dead to God's merciful love and pleads for the forgiveness of their sins" (*OCF* #6). There is a certain confidence on the part of the church that "death is not the end nor does it break the bonds forged in life" (*OCF* #4). The funeral rites are rich with words and signs of hope that this individual Christian will in fact enter into the fullness of life eternal. Yet it is with Christian hope not certainty the prayer is offered. While we celebrate the gift of life lived by the deceased, we do not play God and, therefore, do not attempt to offer that final act of judgment.

Tension has always existed between belief in hope and the grief of the loss of a loved one. Pre-Christian practices point to the custom of wailing and tearing of garments during the period of mourning. The Christian community replaced these practices with the singing of psalms. Yet our tradition often returned to the emphasis that suggested experiences of dread and punishment rather than hope. This tension has always been present in grappling with the mystery of Christian death.

The spiritual bond that exists between those who live the Christian life in the present and those who have gone before is highlighted by spiritual writers throughout the ages. The Church speaks of the communion of saints, the union of those who have entered into the mystery and who we believe in faith now intercede for us. Therefore we both pray for the deceased and pray that those who now enjoy the fullness of eternal life might intercede for the living.

Various local traditions suggest that the Church has always been active at the time of the death of one of its members. The pressures of modern society, particularly its emphasis on the individual and its attempt at denial of death, pose particular challenges to the ministry of the Church today. Mega-parishes in

Hello

We sat in the funeral home for over an hour while she related story after story about the wonderful woman who was her mother. As I was leaving she told me, "Everything you said has helped me so much." I searched my mind for the words of wisdom. I had said, "Hello." I guess sometimes you speak the loudest by simply being there.

Baby and pall

Good liturgy touches all the senses, and sometimes the mental pictures that we carry from a funeral liturgy are the most powerful.

They wanted four generations to place the pall in the funeral liturgy for this eighty-three-year-old man. Since the only member of the fourth generation was an eight-month-old boy, we decided his father would hold him while placing the pall.

As she lovingly straightened the pall, the wife of the deceased caressed the coffin. As she did, her great-grandson leaned in his father's arm and gently tapped the coffin. Years later, I can still see this baby's fingers next to his great-grandmother's—a mental image of the heritage of love expressed in this beautiful ritual.

urban and suburban settings with their thousands of parishioners who are often members in name only pose significant problems to parish ministry. This is particularly true of the ministry of the Church at the time of the death of one of its members. Modern funeral practices focus on avoiding death by preparing the body to "look so good!" Funeral homes frequently model their decor on catering halls with elaborate settings and soothing music. Some families even choose to avoid the fact of death altogether by eliminating a wake and moving as quickly as possible to burial.

The *Order of Christian Funerals* suggests a different approach:

> The celebration of the Christian funeral brings hope and consolation to the living. While proclaiming the Gospel of Jesus Christ and witnessing to Christian hope in the resurrection, the funeral rites also recall to all who take part in them God's mercy and judgment and meet the human need to turn always to God in times of crisis (*OCF* #7).

The primary responsibility for ministry at the time of the death of one of its members lies with the Christian community (*OCF* #9). It is the faith of the community that offers support to the individual mourners. Others in the community have shared the grief of this member. So often it is a mother who has lost a child who is the best person to speak to the woman in grief at the loss of her child. One widow consoles another, and the parents of a young man who died of AIDS console the parents of its latest victim. Words of consolation are offered in faith. But these words are not simple pious utterings. They flow from the faith experience of other Christians who have already walked the road of facing the challenge of death.

Along with the responsibility of consoling the mourners with words of faith, members of the community help the mourners with the tasks of daily living. They also assist the family to prepare the funeral liturgy.

Just as the RCIA suggests a process whereby one becomes a member of the Christian community, the *Order of Christian Funerals* offers a series of rites to assist the mourners as they bring their loved one from the moment of death to burial. The various rites provide opportunities for the Church's presence at each moment of the journey from death to burial.

Prayers are provided in the *OCF* for use at the time of the death of a Christian. This is an intimate moment, and yet the Church presumes to be present in at least the presence of one of its ministers. It is appropriate to use this simple ritual rather than to anoint the deceased since the sacrament of anointing presumes some participation on the part of the individual being anointed.

Prayer also provides support at the first viewing of the deceased in the coffin. The *OCF* provides a simple ritual entitled

Gathering in the Presence of the Body. A lay minister might provide this service for the family. In some cases, the funeral director will use this ritual to assist the family at this difficult moment.

Depending on local practice the family may have a wake of one or two nights. The *OCF* provides a vigil service for the evening prior to the funeral Mass. It also provides a similar service of the Word or the Office for the Dead for use on the other evening where needed. The design of these wake services brings together the larger community of family and friends in prayer for the deceased and the mourners. A dual focus of prayer of intercession and prayer of consolation is present in these rituals. At this juncture in the journey from death to burial we have moved from the very intimate setting of immediate family to the larger gathering of family and friends of the deceased. Traditionally a priest or deacon presided over the wake service; however, the *OCF* suggests that a lay member of the community may be called upon to preside at this gathering of the Church.

The transfer of the body to either the church or the final resting place is often a difficult moment for the mourners. Again, a simple ritual is offered to assist the family and friends in their prayer at this time. A lay minister may also lead this ritual that culminates in a procession to either the church or final resting place. This procession with its accompanying psalm assists the movement.

The high point of the Church's rites at the time of death, the funeral liturgy, is typically a Mass, but may also be celebrated outside Mass. Here the entire Church gathers to pray for the deceased and to offer support to the mourners. The challenge to a local community is to catechize its members so that they understand the importance of their participation in each funeral liturgy. Some members of the parish will participate as members of the praying assembly. Others will have specific liturgical roles such as lector, Eucharistic minister, or musician. All will strive to provide the family of the deceased with a prayerful celebration of the Church's funeral liturgy.

Lastly, we bring the deceased to the final resting place where we celebrate the Rite of Committal. This simple ritual of prayer and song brings the journey from death to burial to closure, a journey that church and family have made together.

As is evident, a variety of lay ministries has evolved in the *Order of Christian Funerals.* These ministries might come under the heading of the Ministry of Consolation for it is through the service of such ministers that the Church externalizes its desire to console the mourners. These ministries flow from a new understanding of church where active participation in the Church's liturgy is the right and obligation of all its members. This primary participation is assisted by the service of specific ministers who through their particular responsibilities make full participation possible. The priest who in the past was responsible for all wake services and for the funeral liturgy is now often in a position of training others to ensure that all who are in need of the church's ministry might be served. The *OCF* places responsibility for ministry not on the priest alone but on the priest working in conjunction with lay ministers who are formed with the particular Ministry of Consolation in mind.

Letter from a wife

We had discussed the fact that some families would not want us to do anything. We would still send a cake and card. We would not feel rejected. This was the case one afternoon as I introduced myself to the family of an elderly man. However, since I had taken the time to get dressed up on a hot summer day, I decided to stay for a while and chat. Later the organist and I planned the Mass with the stories I had listened to in mind. Almost six months later, a letter came to me at the church from the family that we "hadn't touched."

"It has taken me a while to write this letter, but I find I am now ready to say thank you. When you first approached me to plan my husband's funeral Mass, I said no. I said something about it being too painful. The truth is I said no because my husband and I had not been to church in a long time—I think you knew that—and I didn't feel I had the right to have a special Mass. I was also embarrassed. I didn't know much about the Mass. I didn't feel worthy, and I guess I was a little afraid God didn't think my husband was worthy, even though he was a good man.

But you didn't give up on me. Instead you sat and encouraged us to tell story after story. I've been studying the Mass booklet. I've read the words to the songs and looked up what was said so I could read it again.

I've come to realize that we really did plan a special Mass for my husband. You took everything we said and chose songs and parts of the Bible that were just right. I feel like the son from your favorite Bible story. The one who was coming home to tell his father he was sorry. Then before he could say anything, his father reached out to him with love.

All of the people from church—the woman who took time to bake a cake for us, all the people who helped us in the church, Father who spoke as though he really knew John and cared about him, and your gentle support made me feel like God was hugging me.

I now have confidence that God treated John the same way you treated me. I know that he is at peace. That's what I'd like to thank you for the most, because knowing that has made losing him a little easier to bear."

2 The Rites from the Perspective of the People Involved in the Ministry of Consolation

"If one member suffers in the body of Christ which is the Church, all the members suffer with that member" (1 Corinthians 12:26). For this reason, those who are baptized into Christ and nourished at the same table of the Lord are responsible for one another. When Christians are sick their brothers and sisters share a ministry of mutual charity and "do all that they can to help the sick return to health, by showing love for the sick, and by celebrating the sacraments with them." So too when a member of Christ's Body dies, the faithful are called to a ministry of consolation to those who have suffered the loss of one whom they love. . . . The Church calls each member of Christ's Body—priest, deacon, layperson—to participate in the ministry of consolation: to care for the dying, to pray for the dead, to comfort those who mourn (*OCF #8*).

The responsibility for the ministry of consolation rests with the believing community, which heeds the words and example of the Lord Jesus: "Blessed are they who mourn; they shall be consoled" (Matthew 5:3). Each Christian shares in this ministry according to the various gifts and offices in the Church (*OCF #9*).

The Community

As the above paragraphs show, the rationale for the parish Ministry of Consolation lies in the understanding that the role of consolation at the time of death rests primarily with the community.

Ministering to the family is not only the role of the priest, but belongs to all who have been baptized in Christ. Within that community, there are specific roles that need to be fulfilled for the ministry to achieve its full impact. Those specific roles within the Ministry of Consolation are outlined on the following pages.

By giving instruction, pastors and associate pastors should lead the community to a deeper appreciation of its role in the ministry of consolation and to a fuller understanding of the significance of the death of a fellow Christian (*OCF* #9).

The Priest

As priests work with the Ministry of Consolation, they quickly find out that far from diminishing their role, the ministry enhances the role and effectiveness of the parish priest. Working with this ministry helps the priest to concentrate on being an effective enabler, or facilitator, of the different gifts in the parish, and he becomes the one responsible for building up the ministry. The parish priest is able to concentrate on the task of calling forth gifts from the community and being the motivating force behind it all. As such, his role is to identify potential leaders and ministers in the parish, to excite them about this ministry, and to offer training in both the theological background and practical aspects. Reminding people of their baptismal call from Christ to serve, the priest is the motivator in getting the ministry going.

Once the ministry is underway, the priest continues to build up the ministry and the ministers through his spiritual guidance and direction. He will have to be the one who is available to the companions and the coordinators, when they are in need of support and guidance in their struggles as they deal with people in grief. He will be available for meetings, prayer experiences, and other gatherings with the ministers, and, most importantly, will offer generous amounts of affirmation and encouragement.

His ministry will reach not only the ministers of consolation, however, but will continue to extend directly to the families in mourning. He will be able to do this more effectively, though, because the companion and coordinator will be taking on much of the nitty-gritty detail work concerning the funeral Mass. The priest will be free to spend time with the family, offering quality healing time and basic grief counseling as might be appropriate in the days after death. The companion can alert him to particular family situations, which in turn can help the priest to be even more effective and focused in his outreach to a particular family. The priest will often find that the Ministry of Consolation facilitates a family's coming to the sacrament of reconciliation during or immediately after the days of the wake. When that happens, the priest is truly then fulfilling one of his primary tasks as minister of Christ's sacraments.

Lastly, the priest of course continues to act in his main role as leader of prayer, particularly as celebrant of the Eucharist. With the assistance of the ministers of consolation, he will find his role as presider and homilist greatly enhanced. Because the ministers handle the details concerning the Mass and tend to directing the family on the day of the funeral, the celebrant has the freedom to truly attend to his role as presider; this results in a greater prayerfulness that really shines through in one's celebration of the Mass. The homily can be a truly personal moment of joining the deceased's life to the life of Christ and the life of the Church, thanks to the input of the companion.

Far from diminishing the role of the priest, then, the Ministry of Consolation enhances his effectiveness and allows the priest to devote his energies to ministering to the larger needs of the parish. At the same time, he maintains a personal presence to and contact with the grieving family, in an even more effective way.

When No Priest Is Available to Preside at a Funeral Liturgy

It is becoming more and more common in some places for a priest to be unavailable to preside at a funeral Mass. In such a

---

Fred

I visited with the family of James Patrick for a number of days. As I sat with his wife that afternoon, I listened to family and friends tell stories. It seemed a little strange to me that a large number of the stories were about Fred. I assumed he was a friend or relative who could not make the trip to the funeral.

After the vigil, I sat with his wife as well-wishers paid their respects. She wanted everyone to meet "the person from my church." Again, everyone discussed Fred. It almost seemed insulting to James Patrick. Finally, when a neighbor remarked how "good Fred looked," my curiosity could take no more, and I asked, "Who's Fred?" They all looked at me a little stunned, and then laughed. It seemed James Patrick had always been called "Fred." How you get a nickname like Fred from James Patrick no one could say, but his wife couldn't even remember hearing him called anything else. "Why" I asked, "didn't you put that information on any of the forms given to the funeral home or the church?" At his baptism, James Patrick was the name used, and his family would never have considered mentioning anything less formal. After all, this was "the Church."

I had already given the presider information for the homily. The next morning, however, I told him about "Fred." While the family would not think it was proper to pray for Fred during the Mass, I felt at some point in the homily, it might be meaningful to use the nickname everyone else used.

The homily for James Patrick was filled with the wonderful way this man had lived out the life of Christ. At the end, the presider said, "And now the Lord calls again to James Patrick when he says, 'Come home, Fred.'"

I have called you by name and you are mine.

case, a deacon or a layperson should preside at the funeral service using the "Funeral Liturgy Outside Mass," #183–#203 in the *Order of Christian Funerals*. The *OCF* makes clear provision for someone other than a priest to preside and specifically mentions the unavailability of a priest as one of the reasons when this rite may be used (#178.2). The rubrics refer to a "presiding minister" instead of a priest. On such occasions, the deacon or layperson would also lead the rite of committal following the funeral service.

As part of the pastoral ministry, pastors, associate pastors, and other ministers should instruct the parish community on the Christian meaning of death and on the purpose and significance of the Church's liturgical rites for the dead. Information on how the parish community assists families in preparing for funerals should also be provided (*OCF* #9).

The Funeral Director

The pastor must meet with all the funeral directors associated with the parish and explain to them the purpose and meaning of the Ministry of Consolation. The funeral directors should understand all the different roles within the ministry. At some point it might be a good idea to arrange a meeting between the funeral director and the companions, so they can get to know each other and exchange information. The cooperation and understanding of the funeral directors are essential since they are almost always the first contact a family makes at the time of death. When arrangements are made, the funeral director can briefly mention to the family the existence of the parish Ministry of Consolation and can explain that they will be contacted by ministers from the parish to help them during this time. This can help "break the ice" with a family prior to the companion's contact.

The Coordinator

Along with the role of the companion (described below), the role of the coordinator is perhaps the most essential one. This is the first person contacted after the call comes to the parish to set up the funeral Mass. The coordinator then "coordinates" all the other ministers and makes sure that all roles are fulfilled. This is a person who should be comfortable with making numerous phone calls to line people up for tasks and who should have the time and availability to deal with return phone calls. This person has to be available to set the process in motion as soon as the parish is notified of the funeral. Usually it is the parish secretary, or whoever is responsible for taking in funerals at the parish, who would contact the coordinator. Although the coordinator "coordinates" all the other ministers for a funeral Mass, this person usually has no direct contact with the family in mourning. Unlike all the other specific ministries, the coordinator might function solely from the home.

Among the phone calls the coordinator will have to make are:

- a companion
- a cake-baker
- ministers for the funeral Mass:
  - lector(s), if needed
  - Eucharistic minister(s)
  - altar server(s)
  - person to prepare the booklet
  - ministers of hospitality (These ministers assemble and hand out the booklets, make sure the church and its entrance are ready, greet guests, and are prepared to place the pall or bring up the gifts if needed.)

Members of the community should console the mourners with words of faith and support and with acts of kindness, for example, assisting them with some of the routine tasks of daily living (*OCF* #10).

The Cake-Bakers

One of the first people to be contacted by the coordinator would be one of the cake-bakers. This is the person responsible for delivering a cake to the home of the family in mourning as soon as possible. A note expressing the condolences and support

Not alone

Her mother had lived with her for the past five years; the last six months with hospice because of her cancer. Every morning at 10:00 she and her mother had coffee together at the kitchen table. This morning her husband and two daughters were shopping, and at 10:00 the house was completely quiet. As she sat at the table, she said to the walls, "I guess I'm really alone."

It was at that exact moment that the doorbell rang and a Ministry of Consolation member delivered a homemade cake with a card offering the condolences of her parish. She was not alone.

In discussing her role in our ministry, one minister said, "Well, I only bake a cake." Only bake a cake!

I stood in the funeral home for hours listening to a deceased woman's children invite everyone home to share, "The cake that the church sent." As I sat at the kitchen table with a family, I watched the father of the deceased come back from the door crying as he said, "The church sent a cake."

Only bake a cake!

Where are you?

I had been away and, therefore, didn't get the call from the coordinator until after 3:00 on Monday for a Wednesday funeral. Since the family was at the funeral home, I left a message on their machine at home. A few minutes later, the funeral director called to ask, "Where are you? The family is eager to start planning." They wanted everything to be "just right," and he had explained that the Ministry of Consolation would be there to help. They invited me to breakfast the next morning, and, together, we planned a short prayer service, Gathering in the Presence of the Body, for

of the parish family accompanies the cake. This is simply a first contact, and no in-depth presence or conversation would be expected of this minister.

Given the importance and meaning of food in human interaction, this first gesture of outreach means a great deal to the family. Depending on the circumstances of the parish, some other food (e.g., a casserole) might be provided. The important part is to make a first contact using food as an expression of concern and to personally deliver a written expression of sorrow from the parish.

Whenever possible, ministers should involve the family in planning the funeral rites: in the choice of texts and rites provided in the ritual, in the selection of music for the rites, and in the designation of liturgical ministers.

Planning of the funeral rites may take place during the visit of the pastor or other minister at some appropriate time after the death and before the vigil service. Ministers should explain to the family the meaning and significance of each of the funeral rites, especially the vigil, the funeral liturgy, and the rite of committal (*OCF* #17).

The Companion

The coordinator assigns a companion to the family. This should be done as early in the process as possible—as soon as the coordinator is notified of the funeral and at the same time as the cake-baker is assigned, if not before. It is the companion who will walk the journey with the family through the days of the wake and who will assist them during the celebration of the funeral Mass.

The first few times a person acts as a companion to a family, there will be all sorts of feelings and reactions to deal with inside oneself. One might have to get past a feeling of "intruding" on a family's private grief; it's not unusual to have the fear that one will be bothering the family. Companions need reassurance that God wants us to console one another, and that far from being an intrusion, this is what community is supposed to be about. Spending time praying before and after meeting with the family will go a long way to helping this experience be open to the guidance of the Holy Spirit, a guidance which will carry us beyond our own fears and limitations.

The companion makes an initial phone contact with the family to introduce herself or himself and briefly explain his or her role. This first contact needs delicate handling, and any reactions from the family should be received with openness and love; it is not a time for the companion to interpret hesitancy or confusion as personal rejection. Remember, for many families this will be the first time the Church has reached out to them in any way like this. They may not be sure how to handle it; they may not know what to make of it. Perhaps they are uncertain of your motives because they have not been to church in many years and are feeling somewhat guilty over that. Companions may even find anger at the Church directed toward them. Don't be put off by an initial reaction.

The companion arranges to meet with the family. The chief purpose of this meeting will be to begin planning the funeral liturgy. This meeting should take place in whatever way is most convenient and helpful for the family. Ideally, it will be at a time and place other than the funeral home during visiting hours— the family is too distracted greeting relatives and friends to give their full attention. Perhaps the meeting could take place at the home of the mourners at a convenient time, or perhaps at the funeral home, but before visiting hours begin.

The companion should not consider his or her ministry to be one of grief counseling; that is something that, while necessary, goes beyond the scope of the Ministry of Consolation, and the need for which arises somewhat later in the mourning process. Of course, the companion should be a person of true compassion who can employ active listening skills. She or he should be willing to meet people where they are, recognizing that often one will have to minister to people who have been away from the Church for a long time. The companion should be secure enough to deal with any anger toward God or the Church, or anger toward death in general, that may surface. She or he should also be prudent and tactful in understanding difficult family situations such as divorce or other discords—situations often exacerbated at the time of death. Also, the companion must always remember that the main goal is to minister to the family and assist them during this time, not to impose his or her own agenda on the family. If the companion has the attitude of trying to "save" or "convert" the family, it will be counterproductive, if not outright harmful. Indeed, profound evangelization will take place simply through the companion's presence and role, even if "churchy" language or spiritual themes are never explicitly mentioned.

Principally, then, the role of the companion is to represent the care and concern of the parish community, to express that concern in word, deed, and simple presence, and, most importantly, *to companion the mourners through the planning and celebration of the funeral liturgy.* The companion will explain to the family the meaning of the different rites, the elements of the rites, and the options available for each of the rites. To assist the family in making these

the young grandchildren that afternoon. We used Psalm 23 from the Children's Liturgy of the Word, and each grandchild told a favorite remembrance.

That night at the vigil service, an extended homily included stories and a favorite song. Everyone had some ideas for the funeral Mass. For this family, the journey of separation was a prayerful experience. I was glad there was someone to answer when they called out, "Where are you?"

Thank you from a daughter

Thank you notes are often received from the families to whom we minister. One daughter wrote, "It meant a great deal to all of us that we were able to say good-bye to Dad in a personal and meaningful way rather than some way predetermined by people who didn't know him. It was comforting, heartwarming and truly amazing that my mother, who is generally so private, opened up to your condolences. You eased her pain, and I will be forever grateful. You have brought me back."

choices, the companion should leave the family with booklets which clearly outline the different options available for readings and hymns. The companion needs enough liturgical background training to be sure that he or she is supporting the rites of the Church, and not simply catering to his or her own, or to the mourning family's, personal whims for what may seem "nice." The options which the companion can guide the family toward in planning the funeral liturgy are as follows:

- opening hymn
- who will place the pall on the coffin*
- placement of any Christian symbols*
- choice of readings, responsorial psalm, and intercessions
- who will do the readings and intercessions*
- who will present the gifts at the offertory*
- offertory hymn
- Communion hymn
- will there be a meditation hymn or eulogy*
- song of farewell
- closing hymn

*Indicates roles which family members or friends can perform in the liturgy if they so choose (if not, these roles should be fulfilled by ministers of consolation or other parish ministers).

Planning by phone

One of the granddaughters of the deceased who was eight months pregnant and living in another state could not come up to the funeral. She was really upset; everybody else in the family would be there. So, her brothers and sisters prepared the Mass over the phone with her; in this way she felt like she was a part of it all. She had a say in all of the choices, and they even sent her the booklet. She felt connected rather than left out.

The family members will not, of course, be able to make all selections at a first meeting with the companion. The goal is to leave the family with materials that they may hold on to, look over, and discuss. As mentioned above, separate booklets may be devised to outline the choices for readings, music, and general intercessions. These booklets may be left with the family members for their perusal. It is in the process of their making these selections that they will hopefully come to an appreciation of what the Church is saying through the readings and hymns. It will give the family the opportunity to reflect on their loved one's life and how that life, as a manifestation of God's love, can be celebrated through the ritual of the Church. Therefore, the companion should plan on having a second meeting with the family to make definite choices after the family has had a chance to read the booklets and to think about their options.

In addition, the companion at this second meeting should spend some time gathering information about the deceased for use in the homilies (or reflections) at the wake service and Mass. Of course, the companion should not give the appearance of "taking notes" during a meeting, but should simply talk with the family about the deceased and then later compile the thoughts in written form for the homilist.

Some information that might be helpful to the homilist would be:

- Names of relatives to be mentioned
- How person died (sudden? long or short-term illness? suicide?)
- Faith-life of person (very active in church? attended Mass? not practicing?)
- Person's occupation, hobbies, interests
- Family's description of person ("good husband," "loving mother," "very loyal and giving person," etc.)
- Other information

In certain instances it may happen that the family does not wish to make any choices at all. Perhaps they are too grief-stricken, perhaps they have been away from the Church and are unfamiliar with the Mass, or perhaps for some other reason they just want to leave it to the companion to make all the choices. The companion should gently try to lead the family to making the choices but should not push too hard or force them. Even if the family makes no choices and the companion has to do it all, the Church is still ministering to the family and providing them with the level of support which they need. We must never interpret lack of involvement as lack of caring but rather respect that different people are capable of differing levels of response when they are in the midst of grieving.

After this second meeting with the family, the companion gathers all the information, organizes it, and rewrites it in a sensible form. The personal information concerning the deceased's life and faith is passed along to the priest who will preside at the funeral Mass. If someone other than the companion will be presiding at the vigil service, a copy of that information should also be forwarded to that priest, deacon, or other minister. The list of selections for the funeral Mass should be forwarded to the person who will be preparing the booklet (see appendix, pages A19 and A20).

The assembly's participation can be assisted by the preparation of booklets that contain an outline of the rite, the texts and songs belonging to the people, and directions for posture, gesture, and movement (*OCF #11*).

The Booklet Preparers and Assemblers

Booklets can be prepared for each and every funeral liturgy. These booklets add a warm, personal touch to each funeral. All options could be available on a computer program or template, and it would simply be a matter of piecing together various choices

The name

Everything went wrong that morning as we tried to put booklets together. As we raced around town trying to find a place that was open with a copy machine that worked since the one at church seemed to be on strike, we couldn't help feeling that maybe we should just skip the booklet today. We were still putting them together as the family pulled up and members of the ministry kept running back and forth bringing booklets as they were finished.

During the opening prayer, I watched the deceased's eighty-five-year-old sister and best friend as she looked down and opened the booklet. Tears came to her eyes as she reverently touched her sister's name. Every moment of the morning was worth it.

"Daddy's Little Girl"

As I sat with the deceased's daughter, her anger was a live thing. For an hour and a half we sat across the kitchen table as I tried desperately to connect with her on some level. She never looked at me. To her, I was the Church. She never looked up. She finally informed me that her mother had died six years, three months, and four days ago, and the Church was responsible for ruining the funeral. She didn't expect her father's funeral to be any different. She wanted two songs—neither of which belonged at a Mass. When I talked with the presider, we decided that one verse of "Daddy's Little Girl" could be played in place of a eulogy. The other could be done right after the vigil service.

As the daughter left the church after Mass she hugged me. I was still the Church, but I was not the same Church.

to design an individualized booklet. Someone with some computer knowledge should be in charge of this aspect, although others with little or no computer background could be trained to do the actual work, so that the task does not become too burdensome for any one person. An outline of what a booklet might look like and the various elements that would go into it along with other sample materials are at the end of this book (pages A21–A24).

The coordinator also assigns a team of volunteers to assemble the booklets. These can be the ministers who will serve as ministers of hospitality, or they can be a separate team of people, solely responsible for booklet preparation.

One drawback with the preparation of the booklets is that the work will have to be done at the last minute because plans for the Mass may not be finalized by the family until the day before the Mass. The people who prepare the booklet off the computer, run off copies, and collate and assemble the booklets will have to get used to doing so with little notice. It would not be unusual for the computer work to be done the night before the Mass and for the collating and assembling to be done the morning of the funeral.

Since liturgical celebration involves the whole person, it requires attentiveness to all that affects the senses. . . . The ritual gestures, processions, and postures should express and foster an attitude of reverence and reflectiveness in those taking part in the funeral rites. The funeral rites should be celebrated in an atmosphere of simple beauty, in a setting that encourages participation (*OCF* #21).

The presiding minister or an assisting minister may quietly direct the assembly in the movements, gestures, and posture appropriate to the particular ritual moment or action (*OCF* #40).

The Companion (same as mentioned above)

On the day of the funeral Mass, the companion sees to the overall smoothness and prayerfulness of the celebration. Each of the ministers (see below) should already have been assigned by the coordinator, and these ministers should arrive knowing what they are to do and how to do it. The companion acts as a central contact person for last-minute arrangements and as a liaison to the presiding priest. Once the family and mourners arrive, the companion supports them throughout the funeral liturgy, assisting them in whatever way will facilitate their prayer.

The companion greets the family members as they arrive at church and introduces them to the presiding priest. With the help of ministers of hospitality, the companion assembles the people at the entrance to the church in preparation for the opening rites and entrance procession. If family or friends are placing the pall, the companion assists them in getting it into place. The companion directs the family in finding their way to their seats during the entrance procession. If family or friends are doing the readings, the companion accompanies them to the ambo and points out the readings. The presence of the companion near the mourners may also signal them when to sit, stand, or kneel during the Mass.

In addition, the companion directs any family or friends who will bring forward the gifts and sees to the proper flow of traffic during the Communion procession (with the help of the ministers of hospitality). Finally, the companion offers farewell condolences to the mourners as they exit the church at the end of Mass. In general, the companion is there to attend to the needs of the family during the Mass, and the companion should be assisted by ministers of hospitality.

In the celebration of the funeral rites laymen and laywomen may serve as readers, musicians, ushers, pallbearers, and, according to existing norms, as special ministers of the eucharist. Pastors and other priests should instill in these ministers an appreciation of how much the reverent exercise of their ministries contributes to the celebration of the funeral rites. Family members should be encouraged to take an active part in these ministries, but they should not be asked to assume any role that their grief or sense of loss may make too burdensome (*OCF* #15).

On the day of the funeral Mass, the following liturgical ministers participate.

The Community

First and foremost is the role of the community whose members are in attendance to pray for their deceased brother or sister and his or her loved ones. This is a powerful sign of the role of the Church. Since funerals are often scheduled at times when many family and friends cannot be there due to work or family commitments, this role becomes especially important. An empty church on the day of the funeral can turn what is supposed to be a celebration of hope and fulfillment into a maudlin exercise. Therefore,

People in church

As I sat in church before Mass, a young family stopped to say hello on their way to their seats. There was nothing unusual about the action except for the fact that I knew this young family had not been to church since the baptism of their last child. His mother had died the week before.

I started looking around the church and counted eighteen people that I knew were not in the Church last year. They were all there because a funeral liturgy had touched their lives and made them feel part of a believing community.

Our parish has numerous evangelization programs calling people back. Yet, the Ministry of Consolation had been at the door to welcome them when they knocked.

all the ministers outlined below, through their attendance and participation, make up a worshipping community that offers presence and support to the family. In fact, this can be a separate ministry in itself: people who do not wish to get involved in other ways but who are daily Mass-goers could make the commitment to attend funeral Masses. Their sole function would be to attend and provide a worshipping presence. As the *Order of Christian Funerals* tells us, "The community's principal involvement in the ministry of consolation is expressed in its active participation in the celebration of the funeral rites . . ." (*OCF* #11). "The full and active participation of the assembly affirms the value of praying for the dead, gives strength and support to the bereaved, and is a sure sign of faith and hope in the paschal mystery" (*OCF* #150).

The Altar Servers

An adult may be assigned as altar server by the coordinator. This is a wonderful way to open up this liturgical ministry beyond children, and a parish may want to consider using adults as altar servers at funerals even if children are available from a parochial school. Participation in this way brings a whole new faith dimension to those who serve. These servers would do all tasks normally associated with altar servers: carrying the holy water, preparing and clearing the altar, assisting with the wine and water, assisting with the incense, etc. Also, altar servers could assist the sacristan in setting up for Mass or be responsible for doing so if no sacristan is available.

The Pallbearers*

If family or friends do not choose to place the pall over the casket, ministers of consolation should be assigned to do this. (Separate ministers to act as pallbearers may be assigned, or ministers of hospitality may also perform this task.) Generally, two people are sufficient. Those who do this will quickly understand what an awesome and holy moment this is in the rite as the community tangibly expresses its love for the deceased by reverently clothing the body with the pall. It is a gesture which should be done prayerfully, slowly, and with great care.

---

*Here, "pallbearers" does not refer to the people who carry the casket, even though this is the usual meaning in everyday conversation. We are using the term in the literal sense of those who will handle the pall, i.e., those who will place the white cloth over the coffin at the beginning of the funeral liturgy.

Christian dignity

In fifty-three years of marriage, they had truly stood beside each other in good times and bad. In the last years her husband had suffered with Alzheimer's. She cared for him at home, always, always working to maintain the human dignity that the disease tried to take from him.

As she placed the pall—slowly, meticulously—the rich symbolism of the sacrament came alive. The human dignity she had maintained in life became Christian dignity as she ritualistically prepared him for new life in Christ.

This assignment is made by the coordinator if the companion informs the coordinator that family or friends will not be doing this. Therefore, this assignment cannot be done immediately, but must wait until plans with the family are final.

The Lectors

Parish lectors should be involved as readers and lead the intercessions if the family or friends are not selected to do these. The companion might in fact want to steer the family away from choosing family or friends to do this. The purpose of the readings is to convey to those in grief the comfort and hope of the word of God; it is a time for the community to reach out to those who are suffering. One might rightly ask if someone who is grieving is sufficiently "present" to oneself and others to be able to do the proclamation of the word full justice. Also, there is the practical aspect that proclaiming the readings demands that one be a good public speaker, a skill that people do not automatically have simply because they are a friend or relative. Remember, the goal is more than just to "read the readings;" the goal is to proclaim the word in its fullness to people who, in their brokenness, need to hear the full power and import of God's word.

This assignment is made by the coordinator if the companion informs the coordinator that family or friends will not be doing this. This is another assignment that cannot be done immediately but must wait until plans with the family are final.

The Music Ministers

It is assumed that all parishes provide an organist and singer for funerals, whether or not they have a ministry of consolation. Therefore, this aspect should not have to be put in place by the ministry of consolation but can be integrated into other structures and procedures. For example, the booklet that gives the musical options should be put together in consultation with the director of music. Each parish can devise its own procedure for informing the music ministry of a funeral—i.e., will the coordinator call the music ministry, will the parish secretary do so as soon as the call comes in, etc.

In all cases the companion should contact the organist and singer to inform them of the choices the family has made. These choices should come from a pre-arranged repertoire. The principles for designing the parish repertoire may be found in *Music in Catholic Worship* and *Liturgical Music Today.* As with other liturgical

"Yeah! I do."

I was surprised to see the deceased's brother at Mass the next Sunday morning since I knew he was a lector in a neighboring parish. After Mass he embraced me and said, "Tell me. Do you believe all that stuff?" I'm sure I looked puzzled since I had no idea what "stuff" he was talking about. "The homily," he said. I wasn't quite sure how to answer and tried to get the attention of the priest who, I was sure, would answer eloquently. Since he was surrounded by people, I simply said, "Yeah! I do." He looked at me for what seemed like forever, and finally said, "So do I."

I knew then how important the Ministry of Consolation was in a parish. I had answered for myself on a very personal level. As a parish we need to say by word and action that we believe in the resurrection. We need to say "we believe" as a community when it may be difficult for an individual to say, "I believe." The Ministry of Consolation says loud and clear, "Yeah! We do."

choices, the music should reflect both the faith of the Church and a pastoral sensitivity to the grieving family.

The Eucharistic Ministers

Some parish Eucharistic ministers may need to be assigned to assist in the distribution of communion. This assignment is made by the coordinator.

The Ministers of Hospitality

Next to the companion, this is the ministry that perhaps leaves the greatest impression upon the mourners. Ministers of hospitality should greet mourners who arrive before the family, hand them the booklet, and direct them where to sit (especially directing them to sit up front, since most people at funerals sit in the back, thereby leaving a large empty space in the middle of the church between the family and themselves); point out where the bathrooms are to anyone in need of those facilities; hand out booklets to family and friends who arrive with the coffin; gather the people in the rear of the church for the opening rites, so that all may see and hear what takes place; assist those in the entrance procession in being seated; help direct movement whenever necessary (e.g., the Communion procession); and in general, assist the companion in whatever way possible to ensure a smooth and prayerful celebration of liturgy.

Ministers of hospitality are assigned by the coordinator, in consultation with the companion who informs the coordinator of the expected size of the assembly and any special needs for which ministers of hospitality would be necessary. This is yet another assignment that cannot be made immediately but must wait for information from the companion.

❧

The ministry of consolation allows for many different levels of involvement, thereby being open to a variety of personalities, gifts, and differing levels of time commitment. There's something available for everyone! Not everyone may feel comfortable working directly with people, but that's acceptable. For those who are, there's the possibility of becoming a companion. For those who are not, there's the possibility of greeting people as they enter church and handing them a booklet. There's also the possibility of simply collating and stapling booklets. Perhaps someone can't

She belonged

Her mother had lived with them in our parish since their marriage twenty-five years ago. For twenty-five years they attended Sunday Mass. After the church was renovated, they had to search for "their seats." When I told the coordinator what Mass they always attended, she called the people who usually served at that Mass to assist at the vigil service and serve at the funeral Mass.

As she left the church, the deceased's daughter thanked me for everything. She told me, "You made me feel like I belong." Her comment stunned me. She had "belonged" for twenty-five years.

be available during the day, but would be willing to sit at the computer one or two nights a week to work on a booklet or would be able to bake and deliver a cake on short notice. However it is worked out, the goal is to have as many people in the parish community as possible involved in this caring ministry.

Addendum:
Future Prayer Service to Gather Families Together

Although the rites don't specifically call for it, a prayer service from time to time for those who have lost loved ones within a specific time frame can bring a further sense of closure for the families and continue the caring outreach of the parish community within a liturgical context.

The prayer service, which could take the form of a vespers service, might be held every four months or so. Written invitations would be sent out to all those families who had celebrated a funeral Mass during the most recent four-month period. The invitations could be followed up with a phone call from the companion who assisted them with the funeral.

The ministers of consolation, especially the companion, would attend the service. Ideally, it would be led by one of the parish priests. Included in the service could be some gesture of remembrance, such as families inscribing the name of their deceased loved one in the parish's Book of the Names of the Dead.

Hospitality and refreshments should follow the service, and this might be the time to offer assistance beyond the ministry of consolation. For example, information about bereavement groups or further grief counseling—either in the form of flyers and literature, or from people actually engaged in those ministries—could be available for those who are interested.

Suicide

The death of someone you love is never easy. When the cause of death is suicide, so many added emotions become part of the grief process.

It was December 21, and I was on my way to visit the family of a twenty-five-year-old woman–daughter, wife, mother–who had taken her life. I could not imagine their pain, and had absolutely no idea what to say. One of the added emotions facing this young woman's family was the feeling that society and the Church would find her unworthy. I decided to let the Scriptures do the talking. I asked them to close their eyes and let the Word of the Lord speak. I read Romans 3:1-9 three times and let the message of love and hope fill their minds and hearts.

During the greeting at Mass both mother and father seemed restless. As the first reading began, they were practically hanging on the edge of their seats. I watched them as the lector said, "For their hope is full of immortality, for God has tried them and found them worthy." When those words were spoken from the ambo, they took each others' hand, and sat back– almost peaceful. The healing process had begun.

This type of liturgical service would be a closing gesture to the family from the ministry of consolation, helping them to move on to another stage in the parish. A sample outline of such a service is provided in the back of this book along with the other sample materials.

Polish woman

She was ninety-two when a stroke left her unable to care for herself and able to speak only the Polish of her childhood. For her son, this was probably the most difficult aspect of her illness. The strong, independent woman who lost her husband over sixty years ago was unable to do anything for herself and unable to communicate her needs to anyone, and she became, in the hospital, just a room number. Since her son and his family were from out of town, visits to the hospital during the six months she was there were difficult and lonely.

When I called, her son politely told me they didn't want to do any of the planning. "Whatever you do will be fine." That afternoon I stopped by the funeral home to visit. There were three mourners. I went back that night and the same three mourners were still there alone. The coordinator got five members of the ministry to join the priest and me the next night at the vigil service. There were still the same three mourners.

Each of us went home and made phone calls for people to attend the funeral Mass the next day. When her son, his wife, and daughter brought her to church the next morning, twenty-seven members of our ministry were present to stand in honor of this member of our faith community and to kneel in prayer with the family who mourned her death. As he left the church with tears in his eyes, her son told me, "You have taken away all the pain of the last six months." This is Church.

3 Adapting the Ministry of Consolation to Your Parish

It is important to remember that what is outlined in this book is intended to be only a *guide*. Obviously each parish will have to take these ideas and make them its own, according to its local circumstances and situations. Your ministry's model—structures, organizational procedures, etc.—will look different from another parish's. This chapter discusses areas that you might wish to be attentive to in setting up your ministry as these areas might demand special adaptation. We will also look at elements that must be common to the ministry in any parish.

Adaptations According to the Size of Your Parish

All kinds of adaptations are possible according to the size of your parish and the number of funerals each year. The more funerals your parish has, the more people you will need involved in order to avoid burnout from people doing too many funerals. A large parish with many funerals will need several coordinators, several companions, and a large number of other ministers so that people will not have to work on several funerals each week. For smaller parishes, a smaller number might suffice. Also, there is the possibility of combining some roles, e.g., people doing more than one function. This can be worked out according to the needs and circumstances of your parish.

Also, the question of rites other than the funeral Mass—the vigil service, gatherings in the presence of the body, etc.—is one that can vary from parish to parish. A parish may well decide that it is not necessary for a priest or deacon to preside at the vigil service, but that because of the connection to the family, the companion is the most logical one to do so. Insofar as a priest or deacon may have several commitments on the same evening, he may not have the time to spend at the service that the occasion might demand. Perhaps another entire ministry will have to be developed in your parish, that of lay presiders. With training, their function would be to preside at these services and work in close cooperation with the companion at the vigil service.

Overall, the most important thing is to find a model that works for your parish.

Elements Common to the Ministry in Any Parish

Enumerated below are some elements that should be a part of any Ministry of Consolation, regardless of the size of the parish or other variables.

1. Anyone involved in the Ministry of Consolation should go through the training sessions outlined in chapter 4. It is essential for anyone involved to have insight into the basic liturgical theology described in chapter 4 and have a working knowledge of the funeral rites as a whole. This is especially true of the companion, who should never be sent out "cold" simply because he or she is a nice, spiritual person. The time of grieving is too important a time in a family's life to try to reach out to them using people who are unsure of what they are doing or why they are doing it.

2. There must be support from the parish priest(s) and proper acknowledgment from the pastor. Words of thanks and appreciation, expressed not only to the ministers privately but also publicly to the parish-at-large from the clergy, will go a long way to offering affirmation and support to those involved in a ministry which is already difficult because of the emotional demands it makes.

3. Proper attire is required for all those who serve in any way at a funeral Mass. This may seem like an obvious point, but it bears stating explicitly. The way we dress is not only an expression of ourselves, but it also expresses the way we feel about those in whose company we are. Dressing up for ministry at funerals is a sign of respect and love for the deceased, the family and friends, and for the ministers with whom one serves.

4. The Ministry of Consolation must not become the private ministry of any one person but must be owned by all. While smaller parishes may have fewer people involved, even in the smallest of parishes this ministry should never be considered the private domain of one person, no matter how qualified or competent that person is. Yes, there will be people in charge and people who act as coordinators, but it is no one's own private ministry. Involvement of many people doing many things is not some nice option; it is an expression of what we believe liturgy calls us to as a community. If one religious or one lay person does it all himself or herself, we are back to something as undesirable as when the priest did it all himself. This is no one's individual project alone.

5. *Remember that ministers always represent the Church, not their own piety.* A funeral is not a time to push one's own spirituality, one's own theology, one's own view of the Church; it is especially not the time to push one's own piety on others. The standard for any and all decisions concerning the funeral Mass and related rites is the official ritual of the Catholic Church as described in the *Order of Christian Funerals.* Other options, adaptations, additions, deletions, etc., should not be made according to the whim of ministers and planners.

6. *Obviously, most of the people involved in the Ministry of Consolation will have to be available during the day and must be willing to be available with little advanced notice.* Usually, daily Mass attendees are a good source of volunteers. They are often willing to attend a funeral Mass rather than a regular weekday Mass if they see doing so as a service that helps someone else. Working out some regular schedule of commitment, some variation of a "day on/day off" rotation with certain people making a definite commitment to be available for certain days, avoids the situation of not having anyone available.

7. *There will be growing pains! As you seek to establish this ministry in your parish, there will be growing pains and difficulties along the way.* The key is to regularly evaluate the whole endeavor. Keep inquiring as to what is working and what is not working; make adjustments and adaptations as you go along. As long as you are adhering to the common elements described in this chapter, the rest is flexible and can be tailored to your parish.

4   Training Sessions

The formation of ministers of consolation is essential; these individuals will represent the Church as they serve those who mourn the loss of a loved one. Not only must the ministers of consolation understand the various rituals that make up the *Order of Christian Funerals* but they must have a good grasp of the church's theology of Christian death coupled with a compassionate and loving approach to individuals who mourn.

The following five sessions are a guide to preparing ministers of consolation for work in the parish. While the responsibilities of individual ministers will vary from the preparation of a cake to assisting the family in the preparation of the funeral Mass, it is suggested that all who will participate in any aspect of the ministry attend all the training sessions. Often an individual who at first shied away from any major commitment will, after attending the sessions, come to realize that the need is great and that with help he or she will be able to accomplish more than ever imagined.

Each of the sessions is based on a two hour period to include time for presentation of content, questions for clarification, and some practicum.

Session 1

Purpose

The goal of this session is to develop the following areas:

1. The mystery of Christian death;
2. The role of the community in the prayer for the deceased and the care of the mourners;
3. The overview of the various lay ministries involved in the pastoral care of the mourners;
4. General liturgical principles for ministers of consolation.

Materials

Each leader and participant should have a copy of:

- The *Order of Christian Funerals*, study edition
- Copies of lesson handout
  - Ministry of Consolation—Description of Ministries (page 45)
  - General Liturgical Principles for Ministry of Consolation (pages 43–44)
- Copies of Reflection (page 46)

Leader's Preparation

- Review chapters 1 and 2 of this book.
- Read the *Order of Christian Funerals*, General Introduction; #1–#7 (touches on the mystery of Christian death); #8–#19 (outlines a vision of community involvement); and #21–#42 (presents an entire section on liturgical principles).
- Review the Questions and Points of Discussion for this session.
- Review the General Liturgical Principles for Ministers of Consolation.

Prayer to begin session

- Opening Prayer (*OCF* #398.7, first sentence)
- Reading—1 Thessalonians 4:13-14 (#13 in *OCF*) Brief reflection on the reading, if desired.
- Intercessions—(*OCF* #392)
- Our Father
- Concluding Prayer (Adapt *OCF* #394)

Leading the Session

1. After the welcome and opening prayer, teach the material on pages 11–16. This will accomplish the first two goals for Session I.

2. Break for coffee.

3. Distribute copies of A Ministry of Consolation—Description of Ministries on page 45.

4. Go over the various lay ministries involved in the pastoral care of the mourners (goal 3) using pages 17–32 of this book.

5. If time permits, distribute and discuss the General Liturgical Principles for Ministers of Consolation (pages 43–44).

6. Distribute as homework, if there is not time to discuss the General Liturgical Principles for Ministers of Consolation (pages 43–44).

7. Distribute Reflection (page 46) for their personal use.

QUESTIONS AND POINTS OF DISCUSSION

The leader of Session I should be familiar with the following questions and points that will likely arise during this first training session. This information represents a deeper understanding of the material, in conjunction with the material throughout this book, that the presenter should have before conducting the first training session.

1. As a companion, how can one best prepare to meet with the family?

Taking time to prepare is very important. First and foremost is preparing in prayer to the Holy Spirit for guidance. Also, get a little bit of background information about the situation from the funeral director before you go in to meet the family for the first time. It's important to have some idea of what's going on.

Another important aspect of being prepared is remembering to just be yourself. We hear so often about the priest being the person of Christ, and this is true. But any baptized person is another Christ, too. In baptism we have put on Christ. We are most truly Christ-like, however, when we are most truly ourselves. If you are being the most authentic "self" you can be, you are being Christ. Our baptism calls all of us to be the human presence of Christ in the many situations of our life. Sometimes you don't think of yourself that way, but that's who you are. You are the Christian encountering the Christian. St. Augustine talks about Christians being what they already are, the body of Christ.

2. What is a good way for a companion to "get into things" with the family?

It's important for the companion to introduce himself or herself as being from the parish, remembering that he or she represents the parish, and the Church as a whole. Say something like, "I'm here to help you plan the funeral liturgy of your loved one, so that it will be a liturgy that she would want." People will respond well when they know you are there to help them come through this period.

3. It's important for the companion to understand his or her ministry as part of a much larger process, or, even better, much larger journey.

Remember, the Church's funeral rites begin at the deathbed. This has always been true of religious communities. No religious sister, for example, ever dies alone. Religious communities have a way of having a whole group of people at the deathbed, and it's a beautiful experience. As sisters or brothers, they have lived the journey together and so they send the sister or brother on her or his way. All Christians have the right to have the Church present at the moment of death, to assist them with prayer. The funeral rites call for the Church to be present at the time of death. The highest point in the process that concludes at the cemetery, of course, is the funeral Mass. As the Ministry of Consolation highlights, there are many ritual moments of opportunity in between. The first of these can be when the family first comes to the funeral home. This is a crucial moment, viewing the body for the first time; it's a traumatic moment for the family. The Church gives a very simple prayer for that time, and one of the ministers from the Ministry of Consolation might be there to do it. There can also be prayers at other gatherings in the presence of the body.

The *Order of Christian Funerals* gives a ritual for such Gathering in the Presence of the Body. It's very simple: an invitation to prayer; a little reading; the Lord's Prayer; a concluding prayer and blessing. At the time of first viewing, its purpose is to help people establish a prayerful context. A layperson can do this ritual with the family, and it is very helpful to some families. It's also a good ritual to use if children are brought to the funeral home for a short period of time. Sometimes there are very elderly members of the family coming for a short time. This is a wonderful ritual to use for them because it's very short, it's focused, and it's prayerful.

A celebration of transfer, a ritual called The Transfer of the Body, could take place if a gathering with the body (for example, at home) and the wake are in two different places. This rite could also be prayed when the family moves from the funeral home to the place of the Mass. It takes the place of the Our Father and the Hail Mary that the funeral director says before closing the coffin. Another minister, perhaps the companion, can do this ritual since the priest has to be in church preparing for the Mass.

There is a certain tension in the funeral home before going to the Mass, and this ritual helps that situation. There is a call to prayer, a short reading from Scripture, a litany, the Lord's Prayer, a concluding prayer, and a call to procession. We pray that God will be with us today as we make this last journey. Chanting the psalm here is the ideal. Perhaps verses could be read as people say their last good-bye at the coffin. The whole dynamic of that moment could be powerful.

At the wake service (the proper name is the vigil), we begin to move to a peak. This service helps us to move from the more intimate moments of the family gathered around the body to the most public moment, which is the funeral Mass. The style of prayer changes according to the public nature. The vigil service gathers family and friends; the Mass gathers the whole community.

We move again to a more intimate setting when those who are the closest to the deceased go to the cemetery. Again, there is a ritual. Throughout it all, it's a process of taking the person along the journey. We look upon the deceased with great respect, and that's part of the Christian way of living into death. We respect the body of the deceased, and we take that body to the grave, with prayer at every step in the process along the way. The moments just mentioned and the rituals of The Office of the Dead are explained and detailed in the *Order of Christian Funerals*.

Again, what we are talking about is a journey. Most of us have become familiar with the *Rite of Christian Initiation of Adults*: we have a catechumenate, a process where it takes anywhere from a year to several years to enter the Church. People go through rituals. It's a real process, a journey. The same thing is happening with Christian death. We don't do this overnight. We don't bury our deceased almost immediately, as Jewish customs dictate. Although some people are trying to force us in that direction with some of the practices they want to impose, we're trying to hold back because there is value in the mourning process.

Remember, the process is for those who are living. The whole Ministry of Consolation is geared to the family members who have to grieve. The minister of consolation looks at the situation of the grieving family and is in a unique position to understand the rituals and the moments in the process that will help the situation of this particular family.

Finally, some thoughts on other options. There is the possibility of the Funeral Liturgy Outside of Mass. We don't want to encourage a Mass if a Mass is not appropriate, and the ritual speaks of the times to use this option. In some circumstances where a priest is not available there would not be a funeral Mass before the burial. If the family is not a church-going family and does not want a Mass, but wants a Christian burial, this would be the form to use. Also listed are certain days in the liturgical calendar when a Mass is not permitted. However, while a parish uses this rite when, pastorally speaking, it fits the situation, it should not be used simply for convenience, e.g., when young members of the family find it more convenient to leave their grandmother in the funeral home and not bring her to the church for a Mass. Be careful about why people ask for something. Also, there is a whole collection of texts for rites of funerals for children. If it is a child's funeral, choose from this body of texts.

There is a richness in the *Order of Christian Funerals* rites. When ministers of consolation get to know them and know what is available, they are more able to meet the varied needs of the families to whom they minister.

4. Remember the connection between the Ministry of Consolation and evangelization.

The whole process that brings the family through the journey from the deathbed to the cemetery is evangelization. Other parish ministries pick up after the cemetery. Formal bereavement groups in the parish can make a contact after the burial or at one of the follow-up prayer services described elsewhere in this book.

At the time of the death of a loved one, individuals are very vulnerable, and because of this, they are also most open to the operation of the Spirit in their life. The Ministry of Consolation can be one of the greatest tools for evangelization the Church has today. More people come back to the Church after they have experienced a funeral with the kind of care and concern on the part of the community that this offers than any other way. We see it over and over again.

5. What about the feeling that this should be a private time for the family without anyone else interfering?

When people are unfamiliar with the Ministry of Consolation they often feel, "People won't want us to interfere. I don't belong there." We have to start thinking in terms of being a minister. Does Christ belong there? Once involved, companions realize that not only do people want us to be there but, after they realize why we're there, they really open up to us. Even if there is initially a "hands off" reaction, when mourners start to think, they often call the companion back to say they have reconsidered. What they don't realize is that it will have an impact on them they never thought would happen. That's what we're looking for: the impact it will have on them, and what it's going to do to them. That's evangelization.

6. Should anyone be a companion?

Not everyone should be a companion. There are people who just should not do it because it is such a sensitive role, and somebody in the parish has to be responsible to make that decision. We suggest the pastor be the one to make these decisions.

7. Is there a conflict between the role of the companion and the funeral director?

No. Funeral directors who see the Ministry of Consolation in action realize that, rather than competing with them, the ministry helps them look even better!

8. Does the vigil service have to be at night?

Yes, we recommend strongly that the vigil service take place the night before the funeral Mass. Many parishes often schedule it for the afternoon because the priest has other things he legitimately has to do at night. That's the great thing about the Ministry of Consolation: it opens up the funeral rites in all their fullness. As the *Order of Christian Funerals* states, it does not have to be a priest who leads the vigil service. When a lay minister presides at the vigil service, the priest can minister to the family by visiting the funeral home at another time. His visit then becomes more personal to the principal mourners. The priest who is going to preside at the funeral Mass should make some kind of contact with the family before the day of the funeral. The companion is a logical choice to preside at the vigil service since he or she has created a relationship with the family. It could, however, be another member of the parish, perhaps people from a team whose ministry is to lead vigil services. The deacon would often be part of that team, but it does not always have to be the priest.

9. What are some options for the family who want a long eulogy?

The eulogy at the Mass is a time for one person to reflect for three to five minutes on the life of the deceased in the context of his or her life in Christ. It could take the form of a simple thank you to all who have come or a song that has great meaning to the family. The telling of stories is an important part of the healing process. Families are often consoled by the ritualization of the life stories of the deceased, and the companion can help them plan these moments. Using the rite, Gathering in The Presence of The Body, some family members could use time in the afternoon to share remembrances. The vigil service is another moment when some time can be spent that would mean a lot to family members and friends. A meal immediately following the burial is another beautiful time for a eulogy, with participants lighting a candle as each member shares a reflection. A *vita* of the deceased could be prepared and distributed to friends at the funeral home in lieu of, or in addition to, a eulogy. This allows the family to have a permanent keepsake of remembrances.

These general comments point to the need to engage each person in the ritual action through attention to the whole person. Engagement of the senses is vital to any liturgical event. Therefore, ministers of consolation need to be able to understand the ritual dynamics of engaging the sensual in the human condition. Art, environment, and music are important elements in any successful liturgical expression. This is certainly true of the funeral rites.

Ministers of consolation must be knowledgeable in Scripture and, in particular, of the lectionary offerings for funeral Masses and other rituals of the *Order of Christian Funerals.* Devote some time and effort to developing the readings offered so that all the ministers of consolation have some understanding of their potential for a prayerful celebration of the rites.

Music plays a very important part in any liturgical celebration but particularly so in the funeral rites where it offers a positive contribution to the prayerfulness of the celebration. It is very important that parish ministers of music understand the role of music in the funeral rites so that they might make appropriate choices for the parish repertoire. In turn, the ministers of consolation must understand the repertoire so that they might be of assistance to families as they make musical choices. As in no other area of liturgy, musical choices can often make or break a liturgy. Although very beautiful, they often indicate a choice for a secular experience. Thus musicians must work closely with the ministers of consolation to assure that the music used in the liturgy is supportive of the Christian endeavor.

Christian symbols are always a vital part of any ritual expression. In the celebration of the death of a Christian this is of primary importance. The liturgy at the time of the death of a Christian should point to the Christ-dimension of the life of the individual. Since Christian symbols should be employed in the rituals, avoid the tendency to highlight the life of the individual rather than the life lived in Christ. When symbols are being chosen to be part of the funeral liturgy, take care to see that they are Christian symbols and that they point toward participation in the Christ life lived by the individual. Avoid anything that would, on the contrary, highlight the individual to the exclusion of Christ.

The *Order of Christian Funerals* points to several symbols that are to be highlighted in the funeral liturgy. The paschal candle, the sign of Christ's ongoing presence, should burn during the celebration of the funeral liturgy. Holy water makes a connection with the baptism of the believer. When the deceased is received at the church, a pall may be placed on the coffin as a reminder of the baptismal garment of the deceased and a sign of the Christian dignity of the person. Incense is used as a sign of honor of the body of the deceased who has become a temple of the Holy Spirit through baptism. The *Order of Christian Funerals* also suggests the use of other symbols during the liturgy. These symbols might be of a more personal nature but point to the Christian commitment of the individual, such as one's rosary beads, a Bible, a medal of devotion, or some related object. Any symbols introduced should not shift the focus from Christ to the individual.

Liturgical principles are important and should not be taken lightly. The Church gives us those principles to help ensure that the mystery we are celebrating is truly centered on Christ. At the same time, we must always balance liturgical principles with a compassionate pastoral response. While we should never cavalierly change those principles, there might be some limited instances when we have to adjust those principles to real-life situations. We have to remember that we are dealing with people in grief—mourners who are in a tender position. We must be pastorally sensitive to their needs. There might be times when, without setting precedent, we can bend on the principles. This should always be done in consultation with the presiding priest. Liturgical planning will involve a careful balance; we must uphold the Church's tradition and the norms of good liturgy, but we must never do so to the point of being too strict and hurting people at the time of the funeral.

Coordinator

- call companion
- call cake baker
- call hospitality group
- call booklet people
- call computer person

Companion

- call family
- visit family
- offer liturgical options
- prepare liturgy with or for family
- discuss liturgy with the priest-celebrant
- lead prayer where necessary:
    - Prayers after Death
    - Gathering in the Presence of the Body
    - Vigil (wake service)
    - Rite of Committal
- call computer person with choices
- call musician with musical choices
- follow-up: visits; telephone calls; cards

Cake-Baker

- bake cake and bring cake with card to home of grieving relatives

Booklet Committee

- companion informs computer person of the funeral liturgy as planned by the family of deceased
- members of the committee run off copies of booklets
- assemble booklets the morning of the funeral (night before when possible)

Hospitality at the funeral Mass

- distribute booklets, seat friends, parishioners, and distant relatives
- companions, coordinators, and booklet people also greet people
- companion meets immediate family and distributes booklets to them

REFLECTION

Inside us are the years we've lived, each wrapped around the last,
a layering that makes us all the sum of what is past.
As you come to this ministry, you bring your death experiences.
Take some time to reflect on them.

When you reflect upon the life and message of Jesus, what is the most helpful aspect for you in facing your own farewells?

What did your community of believers do that consoled you?

What were the things that made your grief journey harder?

What are the images that remain?

Has there been a time in your life when you experienced a process of healing and of recovered hope? How did this happen?

"As they led him away they seized a man, Simon from Cyrene, who was coming in from the country, and they laid the cross on him and made him carry it behind Jesus" *(Luke 23:26).*

How would you feel if you were Simon?

Session II

Purpose	In this session, the presenter will review the Mass of Christian Burial.

Materials

- The *Order of Christian Funerals*, study edition
- Copies of Outline of Mass of Christian Burial (page 52)

- At the conclusion of Session II, give participants:
  - Selection Sheets for Mass of Christian Burial (pages A19–A20)
  - Family Information Form (page A18)
  - Coordinator Information Form (page A17)

Leader's Preparation

- Review Session II—Preparation Points (pages 49–51).
- Read the *Order of Christian Funerals*, Funeral Liturgy #128–#153.

Prayer to begin session

- Greeting
- Reading Luke 24:30-32 (Portion of *OCF* Gospel Readings #10)
- Psalm 103 (*OCF* Responsorial Psalms #6)
- Our Father
- Concluding Prayer

Leading the Session

1. After the welcome and opening prayer, allow time for reactions to and questions about the material covered last week.

2. Explain the various elements of the funeral Mass by going through the Mass with the participants. Refer to, and have them follow along with, #158–#176 in the *Order of Christian Funerals.*

   Use the Session II—Preparation Points (pages 49–51) in teaching material. Distribute Outline of the Mass of Christian Burial Handout (page 52).

3. Distribute the Selection Sheets and Family Information Form (pages A19–A20, A18). Also distribute Coordinator Information Form (page A17).

   Individually or in teams, participants are to plan a funeral Mass with a specific individual and family in mind.

   These planned Masses will be reviewed and discussed in Session III.

PREPARATION POINTS

The Mass of Christian Burial is the high point of the various rites celebrated at the time of the death of a Christian. This celebration is a witness of the community's concern for the deceased and for the mourners. The entire community marks the loss of one of its members and gathers to celebrate the Eucharist, the source and summit of its life. Ideally, the body of the deceased is present in the church during this celebration, taking its place in the Christian community for the last time. Marks of respect are shown to the body both by the sprinkling with holy water and incensations.

Ministers of consolation study the funeral Mass so that they might understand its richness and assist the family in the preparation of the Mass for their loved one. A thorough understanding is necessary so that the minister of consolation might guide the family to make appropriate choices where indicated. This celebration must be able to sustain the dynamic that manifests both that the deceased was a member of a particular family with its unique traditions and of the Christian community with its ritual needs. This creative tension when cared for with a pastoral sensibility permits the preparation of a funeral Mass that supports all present in their grief and challenges them to see death in the light of the paschal mystery.

While ministers of consolation must understand general principles for the preparation of a Sunday Eucharist, the presenter should develop the following special points for companions who will assist others in preparation:

1. Greeting the family and deceased at the door of the church

Some members of the Ministry of Consolation, along with the priest, gather at the door of the church to welcome the mourners and the deceased in the name of the entire community. Here they may place the pall (the large cloth placed on the coffin, a reminder of our baptismal garment) on the coffin or may encourage members of the family to do so.

2. Choice of appropriate music for the procession into the church

Often favorite musical selections of family members are inappropriate to the various ritual gestures they are to accompany. The procession into the church calls for music that supports this difficult moment for the family and yet at the same time assists them in their walk down the aisle.

3. Choice of appropriate readings

Spend time during this second session to familiarize the participants with the particular lectionary readings assigned to the funeral Mass. The very fact that such a selection of readings exists is often a surprise to participants. Explain the wisdom of the Church in preparing a set of readings for its celebration of Christian death. These readings focus in a particular way on this mystery and assist mourners and homilist alike in attending to the role of the paschal mystery in this particular death.

A related topic that often causes difficulty is the question as to the choice of non-scriptural readings. It is obvious when one begins to point to the death of this Christian in the light of the paschal mystery that the readings offered for the funeral Mass must focus on Christ. The funeral Mass is not the time to focus solely on the deceased but rather on the death of this Christian in light of the death and resurrection of Christ. When the companion presents mourners with a collection of readings from the *Order of Christian Funerals*, they will be more apt to select from this corpus of readings than if they are simply asked what readings they might prefer. It is important that ministers of consolation be aware of such materials and have them at their disposal for use in the planning process.

There is also the question of who should read. Some families have begun a tradition whereby a family member must read at the funeral Mass. In the preparation of the funeral Mass, the companion might remind the family that the ministers of consolation are there to be of service and would be happy to provide a lector for the Mass. Some conversation pointing out the emotional state of family members during the Liturgy of the Word might be helpful to the family.

4. The homily

The homily given at the funeral Mass is just that—a homily, not a eulogy. The presider prepares the homily with the family's choice of readings in mind. Nevertheless, the mystery of Christian death celebrated causes all to focus on the death of this particular Christian. The deceased is the focal point for the assembly's meditation on the paschal mystery. Therefore, the homilist must know something about the individual, particularly about how he or she lived life as one of the baptized. The companion must listen to the family and to stories which surface during the wake period and give some personal information to the homilist.

5. General Intercessions

Encourage members of the family to prepare the General Intercessions. As with the readings, offer some guidance for the preparation of appropriate intercessions. Instruct companions as to the nature of this particular prayer form. Encourage them to read articles 45–46 of the General Instruction of the Roman Missal, which is found in the Sacramentary, for a concise explanation of this universal prayer. They will be in a position to encourage mourners to add particular names of other deceased members of the family, to pray for family and friends who are sick, and so forth. A booklet containing sample petitions with the introductory and concluding prayers (see General Intercessions Booklet starting on page A31) gives guidance to those involved in the planning and assures the writing of appropriate texts.

6. The gifts of bread and wine

Some members of the assembly bring gifts of bread and wine in procession to the altar. During a funeral Mass the family often chooses to bring forth these gifts. Companions might suggest this act as a most appropriate one for involving family members in a ritual gesture. They need to understand that mourners often ask to bring up any number of symbolic gifts at this time. Generally these are inappropriate and careful conversation on the part of the companion will steer the family away from such gifts. The liturgy calls for the bringing forth of bread and wine that will be transformed into the body and blood of Christ. Since any number of people may participate in the procession, companions encourage families to have as many members as they wish accompany the bread and the wine to the altar. It is not necessary that each person carry something in the procession.

The mourners may choose appropriate music to accompany this ritual action. The song may refer to the actual act of preparation of the gifts, or it may be a suitable meditation song. Its purpose is to help the participants to focus on the liturgical act in which they participate—the mystery of Christ's self-gift in his paschal mystery made present on the altar.

7. The Communion Rite

Give some attention to the Communion Rite during this training session. First, ministers of consolation need to be aware of the Church's teaching concerning the reception of Communion. Encourage them to learn to listen to the mourners' needs concerning their dispositions for reception of Communion, and alert them to lead mourners to the sacrament of reconciliation whenever it seems appropriate. The death of a loved one is often a moment of conversion for an individual and companions need to be aware of the gamut of emotion often present concerning participation in the Eucharist. Ministers of consolation might spend time in discussion of this dynamic so that they may be neither judgmental on the one hand nor appear to lose respect for the Eucharist on the other.

The family may also choose a Communion hymn. Again, the hymn should be appropriate to the ritual action of the assembly processing to receive the Eucharist. They may also choose an appropriate meditation song for the period after the prayer after Communion.

8. Words of remembrance

The *Order of Christian Funerals* suggests that a member or friend of the family may speak before the final commendation (*OCF* #170). These words of remembrance should not constitute another homily nor should they be an extended eulogy. The prayer after Communion should be said; then the eulogy; then the commendation. If possible, the eulogy should be given from a lectern rather than from the pulpit. Ordinarily, one person familiar with the deceased, not a series of people, spends a short period of time (three to five minutes) recalling the life of the deceased so that all present might experience comfort as they listen.

9. The final commendation

In some situations the rite of final commendation is celebrated at the cemetery. In these instances the Mass concludes with the final hymn chosen for the act of the family processing with the coffin.

When the celebration of the rite of final commendation is at the conclusion of the Mass, the family may again choose from the various options in prayers and songs of farewell.

OUTLINE OF THE MASS OF CHRISTIAN BURIAL

INTRODUCTORY RITES

    Greeting

    Sprinkling with Holy Water

    [Placing of the Pall]

    Entrance Procession

    [Placing of Christian Symbols]

    Opening Prayer

LITURGY OF THE WORD

    Readings

    Homily

    General Intercessions

LITURGY OF THE EUCHARIST

FINAL COMMENDATION

    Invitation to Prayer

    Silence

    [Signs of Farewell]

    Song of Farewell

    Prayer of Commendation

PROCESSION TO THE PLACE OF COMMITTAL

Session III

Purpose

This session will be an actual work session with participants presenting their planning sheets to the entire group. The group will then critique the choices so that all might learn from the experiences of the others.

Included in this session will be conversation on the actual celebration from the perspective of the companion and the dynamics of interacting with the family during the Mass.

Materials

- The *Order of Christian Funerals,* study edition
- Selection Sheets and Family Information Forms, completed by participants since last session and brought back for discussion and review.

Leader's Preparation

- Read Session III—Questions and Points of Discussion (pages 55–58).

Prayer to begin session

- Opening Prayer
- Reading Romans 3:4, 8–9 (*OCF* New Testament Readings #4, Short Form)
- Psalm 23 (*OCF* Responsorial Psalms #1)
- Our Father
- Concluding Prayer

Leading the Session

1. After the welcome and opening prayer, review the choices the participants made in planning funeral Masses. Elicit the sharing of their experiences and feelings as they made choices.

2. Be sure to cover all the elements of the funeral Mass in the course of this session. Let the participants offer critique and commentary on various choices.

3. Use the Questions and Points of Discussion on pages 55–58 to steer the discussion and to provide material for your input.

QUESTIONS AND POINTS OF DISCUSSION

The leader of Session III should be familiar with the following questions and points that are likely to arise during this third training session, after the participants have worked with the rites and have put together a plan for a funeral Mass.

1. Note the importance of sizing up the situation as you are working with people.

Different dynamics in a situation will result in different readings being chosen. Sometimes people will come right out and say things, and sometimes they won't. Sometimes they will obviously be in need of comfort in a situation, but they find it difficult to say so—in the case where a child dies of a drug overdose, for example. In this tough situation, the companion must find ways to offer comfort and must also help the family to see that there is life after death. We live in the hope that this life, even if lived in a difficult way, does give way to life eternal. Prepare companions with readings that will offer the appropriate support if the family needs direction in choosing the readings.

Or, a family might be looking for images that speak of the deceased person's living a life after death with Christ. Or, because Aunt So-and-So really lived the Christian life, the family wants to express that her life was a model. This would be a different approach. Yet another approach would be the comfort of the communion of saints and the Church triumphant. Still another focus could be that God is here with us now, helping us through the grieving process.

In all of the above possibilities, we are dealing with the mystery of Christian death from very different vantage points. What is essential is that the companion must be familiar with all the readings that are possible for the funeral liturgy, so that the companion can provide the proper direction if the family asks for that assistance. More often than not, families will ask for some kind of guidance.

2. Don't forget to inform the homilist at the funeral Mass about all the aspects of the situation that you have sized up!

For the homily to be real to the situation, the priest must know all the information. As one possible scenario, suppose the deceased person was actually a very unlikable person, a fact acknowledged by the family members themselves—cantankerous, nasty, and/or not a church-goer. For the homilist to raise that person up as a living saint in the midst of the community would not ring true. Let the priest know the situation so he can preach to it realistically. This becomes especially crucial in cases of suicide, where extra pastoral care for the family is required.

3. The companion can bring other parishioners outside of the Ministry of Consolation who had contact with the deceased into the journey.

Perhaps an extraordinary minister of the Eucharist visited the deceased. This minister would be able to tell the companion a great deal about the dying person, perhaps even some things the family didn't know. The companion could bring the Eucharistic minister into the planning process saying, "I'd like you to meet so-and-so. She brought Communion to your mother and has some thoughts about your mother's dying that perhaps you'd like to hear."

4. Don't overlook the importance of the choice of the Responsorial Psalm.

The psalm choice should come out of whatever the emphasis is going to be in the readings.

Remember too that the musical setting is just as important as the choice of text. Think of the meaning the words of the response will have as people sing them over and over again at the Mass.

5. The General Intercessions (Prayer of the Faithful) can be formulated in light of who the person was.

Intercessions that speak to the deceased being nourished at the table of the Savior would ring hollow if the deceased never, ever went to Mass. We might think that it's just a petition that isn't important, but families will really struggle with something that is said if it's just not true. Don't take anything for granted; what to us is a very small thing can be a really big thing to the family. Be sensitive to that.

In a petition that mentions the friends and family members who have gone before us, the opportunity arises to bring in the whole communion of saints. Mention the names of other funerals the family has been to. Who are the people the family remembers and talks about whenever they get together? Make sure to include those names. It brings that great sense of union that is part of the mystery of the Christian faith.

What else has the family celebrated in the church where the funeral Mass is being held? Marriages? Pray for the couple who started out their married life here. How many people can realistically be mentioned? Quite a few; this is the place to do something like this.

Other names that can be prayed for are those who cannot be in attendance because of illness or travel, or those who gave care to the deceased during the illness.

Remember, though, these are meant to be prayers of intercessions, not prayers of thanksgiving. The wording of the petitions must speak to the reality of intercessory prayer, not thanksgiving. The pattern, however, need not follow the universal pattern used on Sundays. In funerals, as in all of the sacramental rites, the petitions are geared more specifically to the particular celebration and to the needs of the particular community. That's why it's important to follow the suggestions in the *Order of Christian Funerals*, beginning on page 356.

6. Pay attention to the rhythm of the ritual; note the movement throughout and help the family to make appropriate choices.

We start at the door of the church. We greet the people at the door of the church and then the movement begins with the sprinkling with holy water and the placing of the pall. Any number of family members can get involved in the placing of the pall. At this difficult moment, this ritual can really help the healing process. It is something young or old can do. Consider anyone who is going to somehow benefit from the action.

After the pall is on, the choice of the entrance song becomes crucial. The song brings the body and chief mourners into the church. It's a tough moment to walk down that aisle. Hymns can be in the wrong place! As an example, "Ave Maria" is an appropriate musical choice for a funeral, but not for the entrance. At the entrance, we walk in to begin the celebration of the mystery of life in Christ. "Ave Maria" focuses on Marian devotion. It has a place in Christian tradition, but should be at a time of meditation in the Mass—when, for example, you can meditate on the fact that it's been played at every family anniversary.

When a choice is not in the appropriate place, use tact. Don't just say, "We don't do that." Suggest we "find an appropriate place," keeping in mind that the appropriate place could be the vigil service.

We're in the door, at our seats, and we listen to the word of God. The next time a question of movement comes up is at the preparation of the gifts. If only the bread and wine are brought up in the procession, remember that any number of people can be in the procession. Not everybody has to carry something. People accompany the two who are carrying the bread and wine. This is a wonderful place for children in the liturgy.

The family could even bring forward things like the altar candles and altar cloths, and set the table. The companion leads people through this procession, accompanying them and showing them what to do. The companion should walk out of the pew, bring them out, bring them to where the gifts are, hand them what they will be carrying, line them up the way you want them, and send them or lead them down the aisle. The companion is there to make sure the people know what to do and that they are comfortable doing it.

The presence of members of the ministry enhances the movement at the time of the Communion procession.

At the final commendation we, the Church, take leave of the deceased. In the final commendation, there is an invitation to prayer and often an incensing of the body. It's at that time that we sing a very short song. The song speaks to the fact that the person is going forth from us. The recessional procession follows immediately. It is appropriate to sing at the incensation and the recessional. Think about the emotions going on: singing both songs gives people a little bit of time to come to closure.

7. What about questions of culture, such as singing "Danny Boy" during the funeral Mass?

We have to be careful how we handle such requests. Culture and religion are often wed. One is an Irish Catholic, an Italian Catholic, a Polish Catholic, a Haitian Catholic. The most appropriate place for this kind of request is at the vigil service. We always have to be sensitive. If everything else about the liturgy is speaking about Jesus Christ, there is more room to bend at one point. It's always a question of balance, and we walk a very fine line. These questions should always be discussed with the presiding priest.

8. What about reception of Communion?

This is where the non-practicing question comes up—who's going to receive Communion? The companion should try to get a sense of this when working with the family so that the priest can be informed, e.g., "Tomorrow there's going to be a large crowd at the funeral, but I have a sense that no one is going to receive Communion." Or, you may have worked with the family to the point where they're going to ask the priest to come to the funeral home and they're all going to go to confession, and the funeral Mass will be the occasion of their second communion! The companion should also inform the priest if someone is not capable of coming out of the pew to receive Communion so that Communion is brought to them.

During the days of the wake, it's a good idea for the companion to bring up the issue in a very general, non-threatening way: "In preparing for the Mass tomorrow, we just want an idea of whether you think very many people will be receiving Communion." By raising the issue, it eliminates fear and confusion in people's minds.

9. Can there be a meditation song or eulogy after Communion?

Yes, but be careful that this part doesn't overpower the liturgy. If the family chooses, either a post-Communion meditation song or words of remembrance (a eulogy) are appropriate—not both. The sense of appropriate rhythm of the liturgy has to be maintained. Many people often want to say a word or two, and after Communion is the time for it, but it should be only a minute or two. The liturgy can get bogged down if someone talks for ten minutes, so talk to the family in advance since it's hurtful to stop someone once he or she starts.

Session IV

Purpose

This session may be divided into three parts, each of which concerns some aspect of the vigil service:

Part I   A general understanding of the vigil service

Part II   Small group preparation of a vigil service

Part III   After ministers of consolation have had some time to prepare an actual vigil service, the remaining time may be devoted to actual role playing of a vigil service.

Materials

- The *Order of Christian Funerals,* study edition
- Copies of Outline of Vigil Service Handout (page 65)
- Copies of Presiding at the Vigil Service (page 64)

Leader's Preparation

- Review Session IV—Preparation Points (pages 61–63).
- Read the *Order of Christian Funerals,* Vigil and Related Rites and Prayers, #51–#68.

Prayer to begin session

- Opening Prayer
- Reading 1 John 3:1-2 (*OCF* New Testament Reading #15)
- Psalm 148 (*OCF* Responsorial Psalms #4)
- Our Father
- Concluding Prayer

Leading the Session

1. Begin with welcome and opening prayer.

2. Present the material for a general understanding of the vigil service (Session IV—Preparation Points, pages 61–63).

3. Coffee break.

4. Have the participants break into small groups to plan and prepare a vigil service, using #69–#81 in the *Order of Christian Funerals.*

5. After the vigil services have been planned, spend time role-playing the vigil service. Have participants preside, read, etc., and discuss the experience.

PREPARATION POINTS

A General Understanding of the Vigil Service

The vigil service, typically celebrated the evening prior to the funeral Mass, provides an opportunity for friends and family to support one another in prayer. "At the vigil the Christian community keeps watch with the family in prayer to the God of mercy" (*OCF* #56). The Church is present particularly in those who come to minister to the family and friends of the deceased as presider, assistant, cantor, and lector. If we are a community in prayer, then the ministry of consolation is involved in this prayer just as it is in any communal prayer. Ministers of consolation may preside at the vigil service as well as serve in the other liturgical ministries and should study the rite with this participation in mind.

Music

The ritual calls for an opening song. Singing in the funeral home depends on the setting and on the family. Perhaps your parish music ministry could help. The responsorial psalm is another place where you can do some music and some singing.

Readings

The vigil service affords an additional opportunity for the family to choose readings. Some members of the family may wish to read. Where this is not the practice, a member of the ministry of consolation might do so. There are people in each parish who can use their gift of voice for the prayer of the community. The ideal of a diversity of ministries should be evident in the simple prayer. It would be unfortunate if one voice did all the readings, prayers, responses, etc.

Homily

The vigil service calls for a brief homily on the readings. If the companion is the presider, a reflection is given by the companion. While the ritual doesn't call for it in the outline, it does suggest in the notes that it's possible for people to do some kind of eulogizing or story telling at the wake. Just as the gospel is the telling of the story of Christ, so too at the vigil service we can encourage the family to tell stories about the life of the deceased, for the same purpose as listening to the gospel: to build up the body of Christ. The stories are somewhat motivational to the people there, and often the stories are very helpful to the young people present. Young people can hear the model of the life of this person whom they love dearly. We want to allow people to express what's inside them; that's good liturgy. People often feel more comfortable in the setting at the vigil service than they would in the church. There is also the leisure that it can take an hour, if need be.

This is also the opportunity for the family to be more creative: perhaps a poem read; an extended eulogy; a special song; or participation by younger children. The companion can help the family use these moments at the vigil service rather than the Mass. In the Mass we do those things that are important to all of us as a Church. The funeral home or a family member's home after the burial is a beautiful time for things that are unique to people as an individual family. If we incorporate things that are unique to this family into the Mass, we diffuse attention away from the central mystery of Christ's dying and rising.

Intercessory Prayer

Intercessory Prayer is an important element in the vigil service. The family may wish to make appropriate choices from the various options offered and to add petitions that may be of a more personal nature for the family.

The time of the vigil service

When we looked at the overall rhythm from the time of death until the time of burial, we noted that the vigil service comes the evening before the Mass. It's a time when family, friends, business associates—people who have a direct relationship to the deceased—come together and vigil. So, the very name tells us that it's supposed to take place the night before. The reason the afternoon is not the most appropriate time is that the purpose of this is not simply to say the prayers for the deceased alone. As with all of our funeral rites, the purpose is to pray for the deceased and to bring comfort and support to the mourners. In the afternoon, the mourners will very much appreciate a personal visit from the priest. He should still go in the afternoon if his schedule demands that he go in the afternoon. Maybe he could hear confessions if that's what the people want. He could spend some time in one-on-one conversation. Then, in the evening, someone else could go and preside at the vigil service. That's why the Ministry of Consolation encourages the development of people who are going to preside at vigil services. The purpose of the vigil service is to bring together that group of people who gather there the night before; it's not simply to "say prayers." While there is nothing to prevent a priest being present in the evening to preside at the vigil service, if he is able, other ministers should be there as well to fulfill other liturgical roles, e.g., a reader and a leader of song.

Exceptions?

Are there exceptions to the vigil taking place in the evening? Of course. Prayers are not said for the sake of saying prayers. The prayer is for the people who gather. Perhaps you are dealing with a group of senior citizens who all come in the afternoon, and virtually no one will be present in the evening. The prayer should take place when those individuals can gather. It all rests in the companion's ability to think through, "What will be the best thing for this person and this family?" People involved in liturgy have to think of the people who are in need of this prayer.

Keeping other organizations in mind

The Church, in the person of its ministers, gathers in the funeral home because that's typically where the wake is held. The church gathers to pray with the mourners, and we vigil. The tradition of wake services points to any number of people getting involved. Organizations like the fire department, the Knights of Columbus, the Rosary Society, the Daughters of the American Revolution, etc., have a service, and the companion, knowing or asking questions, might be able to work with these organizations in planning the service. Having one prayer service after another tires rather than comforts the mourners. All the societies can be brought together rather than do a completely different prayer service.

It's important that we do the vigil service as called for in the *Order of Christian Funerals*. If the family has a tradition of saying the Rosary, try to fit the Rosary into the vigil service. Instead of a whole Rosary, maybe a decade of the Rosary could be done. Nevertheless, we should do the vigil service. The experience of the vigil service is very rich and very supportive of people's needs.

Involve the family and the community

The image we want to create at the vigil service is not that of one person reading from a book and saying prayers (whether that person be a priest or a companion) but the image of everyone sitting there praying. In order to do that, the vigil service should involve all of the ministries. Of course, this is an ideal, but we should strive for it. We should strive for a service that has a team of people who go in and lead the prayer for the mourners: a presider, a reader, maybe a musician, even an assistant if necessary. Just as the companion took time to go over each of the pieces of the Mass, the same can be done for the vigil service. Will this be done with every family? Perhaps not. But the Ministry of Consolation should be prepared to do it in situations where the family really wants to do everything that's possible to make this the most prayerful experience it can be.

Include the vigil service in the overall planning

Since there is often only a span of two or three days for the companion to work with the family, it is not always possible to plan with them all the rituals in the *Order of Christian Funerals*. However, people will make time for the companion. Once the Ministry of Consolation catches on in the parish, people begin to hear about the ministry even outside of the church structure, and when a death occurs in their family, the idea of a companion helping is not totally new. Also, the funeral director will tell them about the Ministry of Consolation, informing them that somebody from the church will be calling. The companion can meet in the church, the funeral home before the wake begins, or, if invited, in the family's home. Sometimes the mourners are by themselves in the afternoon and delighted to have the companion come. People will make the time when the result is a funeral that says, "This person I love is special."

PRESIDING AT THE VIGIL SERVICE

The environment of the vigil service, generally speaking, is the funeral home. The focus is the coffin. The ministers should not stand in front of the coffin. The body is there as a symbol to us of the life of this person, so the ministers should not put their back to them. Stand off to the side, including the deceased in the prayer. Typically, the mourners are seated. Encourage other friends and family to gather around the mourners for the prayer. The vigil is not simply saying some prayers; it is leading the community in prayer.

A beautiful book to preside from says a great deal. Choose the place you preside from carefully. If you see that they have set up a little section with a picture, stand right there. Choose a place that's really attractive. Stand where everybody can see you. You will be the focal point even though you may not want to be; remember it's not you, it's Christ. Be Christ for these people. You are Christ, come to be with them and you should stand in their presence in such a way that they can focus on you.

When you arrive, introduce yourself to the chief mourners. As you begin, greet the gathered assembly. Some kind of badge makes it clear who you are and that you represent the parish community.

As you go through the greeting, people may not know the proper responses. If nobody answers "And also with you" or other responses, don't yell out the answer; just move on. If you have brought a few people with you, they will respond. Encourage people to stand and to sit as the ritual calls for it.

Throughout it all, be sure your stance is one of prayerfulness. Everyone has to find his or her own way to do this, but your body should be bringing the people there into prayer. Just as there's a rhythm to the ocean, there's a rhythm to the liturgy. The gentle rhythm engages people in prayer and gives them a sense of peace. Rushing can become a distraction to prayer. If the psalm is not going to be sung, it should be read almost musically.

Remember to read through all the prayer texts that are given as options, finding the ones that are appropriate to this situation. Don't just keep using the same ones over and over again.

OUTLINE OF THE VIGIL SERVICE

INTRODUCTORY RITES

    Greeting

    Opening Song

    Invitation to Prayer

    Opening Prayer

LITURGY OF THE WORD

    First Reading

        Reading:

        Reader:

    Responsorial Psalm

        Psalm:

        Psalmist:

    Gospel

        Reading:

        Reader:

    Homily

PRAYER OF INTERCESSION

    Litany

    The Lord's Prayer

    Concluding Prayer

CONCLUDING RITE

    Blessing

Session V

Purpose	This session is divided into two major areas with time for preparation and practicum for each area: the committal service, and follow-up evenings of prayer for the bereaved.
Materials	• The *Order of Christian Funerals*, study edition • Copies of the Rite of Committal Outline (page 70)
Leader's Preparation	• Read Session V—Preparation Points (pages 68–69).
Prayer to begin session	• *Book Of Blessings*, Order for the Blessing of Those Who Exercise Pastoral Service, II. Order of Blessing with Celebration of the Word of God.

Leading the Session

1.   Begin with welcome and opening prayer.

2.   Distribute Rite of Committal Outline. Present the material in Part I: The Committal Service in the Session V—Preparation Points (page 68).

3.   Coffee break.

4.   Present and discuss the material in Part II: Follow-up Evenings of Prayer for the Bereaved in the Session V—Preparation Points (page 69). Include a presentation on Morning Prayer and Evening Prayer (*OCF* #348–#395).

5.   Allow time at the end of the session for overall questions, reactions, and discussion of actually getting this ministry started in a parish.

PREPARATION POINTS

Part I—A General Understanding of the Committal Service

While the funeral Mass provided an opportunity for the entire parish community to pray for its beloved deceased and to support the mourners with their presence and the vigil service provided an opportunity for friends and family to support one another in prayer, the committal service provides a prayerful context in which those who mourn might be comforted as they leave their loved one at the place of final repose. The Church, in the person of its ministers, is present leading the mourners in prayer.

The Rite of Committal is another place for involvement of the ministers of consolation. The minister conducts the service at the grave, the chapel, or the mausoleum. The ritual is designed for that final place where the family leaves the body; it has about it a real sense of finality.

The prayers in this ritual get into the stuff of going into the earth, and, therefore, clash with our tendency to try to avoid the reality of death. People sometimes try to avoid that, but avoidance is not always helpful. We often try to sanitize death too much. The reality is we are leaving the loved one's body in the cemetery. What this whole rite is doing is what any good symbol has to do, namely, maintaining the tension of the ambiguity of the reality that it represents. What we're dealing with here is the mystery of Christian death. Sometimes we're going to hear it and understand it from one angle, sometimes from another. If we're not always clear, the rite is working since we don't know. The rite is holding the tension of the mystery: we are bringing this body here and we don't know everything about the afterlife. We reverence the body as the symbol of the person, and we believe that we will rise again. We believe that this body is more than just the stuff of the physical and how that all comes together is part of the mystery. The ritual has to hold that tension.

The *Order of Christian Funerals* contains two forms: the Rite of Committal and the Rite of Committal with Final Commendation. The difference between those two has to do with when the burial takes place in relation to the funeral Mass. Ordinarily the final commendation comes at the end of the funeral Mass, and then the people move on to the cemetery for the rite of committal—all in one morning, for example. However, more and more we see situations where, for any number of reasons, there is time between the two. In a situation where the Mass is in one state and the burial in another, the ministers may then meet the mourners at the cemetery. In this case the Rite of Committal with Final Commendation is appropriate. Perhaps in the future we will have the funeral Mass at night, and then the next morning people would go from the funeral home to the cemetery.

The structure of the Rite of Committal is quite simple, and this is the ritual the Church is suggesting. It begins with an invitation to prayer, as do all rituals. The invitations to prayer are addressed to the people to bring them into prayer. A short Scripture verse follows. Again, it might be helpful if more than one person went to the cemetery to share the prayer; someone else could do the Scripture verse. The prayer over the place of committal follows the Scripture verse. Notice the different options here; make your choices according to what the reality is.

There is the actual committal. If it is a cremation, you commit the whole vessel to the earth; you don't spread the ashes. This could be done in the chapel or at the burial site.

The intercessions used will be somewhat different from the ones used in church. Together we pray the Lord's Prayer followed by the concluding prayer and a prayer over the people. This is a prayer for the mourners. Notice there is a form for a minister who is a priest or a deacon, and one for a lay minister. Then the people are dismissed. Often there is some sign of farewell, such as placing a flower on the grave.

Remember, people are not there just to hear or say a couple of prayers; people are there to pray about what is happening. The prayers really have to speak to that moment.

Part II—Follow-up Evenings of Prayer for the Bereaved

Follow-up is very important. The relationship established through the time of the funeral shouldn't end there. Without a doubt the family members have had a very good experience with the kind of energy and effort you have put into things, so they are ready to continue to pray with the Church. People come back to the Church as a result of the kind of effort you put into their funeral.

Ministers of consolation are often invited back to the house or to some type of meal after the burial, and they should go if time permits. This is an opportunity for evangelization. In spending this time, you will often find people who haven't been to church in a long time. They will ask you what the Church is like. Good things can be accomplished here.

Follow-up must involve prayer. You may have a bereavement group in the parish who goes and meets with the families, or the bereavement process might be part of the Ministry of Consolation. This will depend on the structure of the parish. Regardless, it is also necessary to have some kind of ongoing prayer structure. People who may not want to come to group meetings or may not want to get together with other grieving parishioners will come to some kind of prayer service. These can be structured to be held every month, every three months, every six months, or whatever. In our Addendum to chapter 2 of this book (page 31), we describe these Prayer Services to Gather Families Together at a Future Date. Please refer to page A27 for a description of how this service could be run.

What is crucial with this prayer service is for the people to know that the Church is continuing to think about them and that we want them to come for a special prayer. If people come to this service alone, the companion is there for them, to walk up with them to sign their names. We really are supporting people with this. Bringing people together after a few months really helps them in the healing process. When the prayer is over, have some kind of hospitality. This again provides the opportunity to talk to people and to reach out to them on their journey toward resolving their grief.

In addition, many parishes do something to celebrate All Souls Day; often this liturgy involves the reading of all the names of the deceased over the past year. Be sure people are invited to that. This All Souls Day experience provides more ongoing contact, so that people are kept in the process with prayer. Asking people to sit through a prayer service is non-threatening, and most will respond well to it.

It's important to establish a pattern for your parish that will become a local tradition.

RITE OF COMMITTAL OUTLINE

Invitation

Scripture Verse

Prayer over the Place of Committal

Committal

Intercessions

The Lord's Prayer

Concluding Prayer

Prayer over the People

Conclusion

Evangelization Through the Ministry of Consolation

With all the talk of evangelization in the Church today, one quickly realizes that the Ministry of Consolation is "primary evangelization." It directly brings the comfort and power of the Gospel to people through a community that is ministering to them and giving witness to what it believes about Christian death at a time when people are very receptive to it. Parishes often spend great amounts of time, energy, and resources devising and implementing programs of evangelization. The focus of these programs is the goal of creating a warmer, more hospitable parish that better meets the real needs of the people. Sometimes, though, in this attention to formal programs of evangelization, obvious avenues which are already in place and can be readily tapped are overlooked. The celebration of the funeral rites is one of these avenues. What good does it do to talk about one's parish being a place of celebration, healing, and liturgical nourishment when the rites themselves do not strive to convey that message? The time of a funeral is a "ready-made" and unparalleled moment to powerfully reach people. The potential for this ministry to transform peoples' lives and spirituality is enormous, and how it reaches out to the bereaved should be obvious.

What is perhaps not as obvious, yet is just as real and as powerful, is the way this ministry affects the ministers themselves, and the role this ministry plays in the development of their own faith.

Those who minister in the Ministry of Consolation speak about a greater sense of belonging to the parish and a greater ownership of the parish's mission to reach out to others. They feel very good about being instrumental in helping to bring others back to the Church since it is not unusual to hear of a family member or friend deciding to return to Mass after witnessing a funeral at which the Ministry of Consolation participated. The ministers also feel very positive about being able to be present to their sisters and brothers in the parish and that others notice the care they give to each element of the ministry.

The affirmation expressed by the families to the companion and the other ministers is a moment of evangelization as well. The fact that people express their appreciation for the work these ministers do opens a whole new dimension to the ministers' understanding of the effect they are having on people. Ministers gain a deeper appreciation for the priesthood of the baptized as they take responsibility for the work of the parish in this way and see that they do make a difference.

It is not unusual for ministers to find their own faith strengthened and for them to gain a deeper appreciation of the theology of Christian death. Through their ministry to the families, through their presence and participation in many funeral liturgies, through their familiarity with the Scriptures and reflection on funeral homilies, ministers speak about a deeper comfort and understanding they have of the mystery of death. They find their faith affirmed and can deal with the death of someone close to them in a whole new way. It is not unusual for the ministers to begin to plan their own funeral liturgy (even though there is no reason to expect that the event will occur anytime soon)! They often become adept at choosing their own Scripture readings, hymns, and other ritual elements, using subtle nuances and a heightened liturgical awareness in making these choices. This too is evangelization. In helping them to explore the reality and mystery of their own death, they come to see death from the deeper faith perspective and within its context as a part of the life of the Church.

This evangelization does not stop with the lay volunteer ministers, however; it can also affect the clergy and professional staff, as well. Priests themselves can be evangelized as they perform their ministry in cooperation with other ministers of consolation. Their homilies can be renewed, and their reflection in preparation for these homilies given new life, since they are now preaching not only to the family in mourning but also to a community who attends funerals regularly. This can provide a wonderful challenge to the priest to avoid "canned" homilies; he can be strengthened in his ministry of making the word of God come alive as he seeks to combine the uniqueness of the deceased's life with the Church's faith about death. The priest may find that his skills as a presider at funeral Masses are enhanced also since he can preside over a liturgy that is reflective of the involvement of the community, rather than over one which is his to do alone. Finally, the priest can find his own spirituality enriched as he listens to the stories and reflections of the companions and others who deal with the families; he can gain insight into human suffering and sadness that will in turn deepen his effectiveness in dealing with people in those situations.

This evangelization can also extend to other professional staff people, i.e., the music ministry, sacristan, etc. Working together can achieve a new understanding, and the boundaries of "turf" can begin to break down when this is seen as a corporate, communal endeavor. A greater appreciation for the ministry of the parish as a whole (rather than "this is my thing, this is your thing") can develop, leading to an expression of mutual support and shared concern which would be a visible sign of the parish's commitment to witnessing to the kingdom of God.

The Ministry of Consolation ministers to all those involved in it as much as it does to the grieving. One of the most powerful values of this ministry as a tool for evangelization is that the community is doing it; this value must never be lost. While it might become easier for one highly organized and motivated person to simply do everything (especially in smaller parishes where the number of funerals would permit this), the whole point is that the ministry does not devolve into one person's "thing." Yes, there is a need for an overseer, be it clergy, religious, or layperson, but an individual cannot do this as her or his project alone. The rites clearly call for the involvement of the larger community.

Appendix

*You are called
to a very
special ministry.*

*"If one member suffers in the
body of Christ which is the Church,
all the members suffer with that member."*
1 Corinthians 12:26

For this reason,
those who are baptized into Christ and
nourished at the same table of the Lord
are responsible for one another.
When a member of Christ's Body dies,
the faithful are called
to a ministry of consolation
to those who have suffered
the loss of one whom they love.
You are called to participate
in a ministry of consolation:
to pray for the dead;
to comfort those who mourn.

INTRODUCTORY MEETING

ON _____

AT _____

IN _____

Your response would help us
prepare our hospitality.

Fold Line

Fold Line

Dear

Our parish is in the process of developing a ministry of consolation to assist our parishioners at the time of the death of a loved one. The thrust for such a program grows out of the revision of the *Order of Christian Funerals.*

Since you play such an important role in the process at the time of death, we invite you to join your fellow funeral directors, the parish priests, and some members of the ministry of consolation for a short presentation of the program and for questions and clarification. Our hope is that your participation in this one-hour meeting will give further direction to us and be of benefit to you as we work for the good of the people of our parish.

The meeting is planned for _____

from _____ to _____

in _____

Sincerely,

Pastor

A Ministry of Consolation: Involving Your Parish in the Order of Christian Funerals

Dear Lector and Eucharistic Minister,

We are in the process of developing a ministry of consolation in our parish to assist our parishioners at the time of the death of a loved one. The thrust for such a program grows out of the revision of the *Order of Christian Funerals*.

The *Order of Christian Funerals* states: "At the death of a Christian, whose life of faith was begun in the waters of baptism and strengthened at the eucharistic table, the Church intercedes on behalf of the deceased because of its confident belief that death is not the end nor does it break the bonds forged in life. The Church also ministers to the sorrowing and consoles them in the funeral rites with the comforting word of God and the sacrament of the eucharist" (*OCF* #4). Not only are these strong words, they are sound words. They speak eloquently of the part you play in the process at the time of death.

The rites call for the participation of our parish community. "Those who are baptized into Christ and nourished at the same table of the Lord are responsible for one another. . . . When a member of Christ's Body dies, the faithful are called to a ministry of consolation to those who have suffered the loss of one whom they love. . . . The Church calls each member of Christ's Body—priest, deacon, layperson—to participate in the ministry of consolation: to care for the dying, to pray for the dead, to comfort those who mourn" (*OCF* #8).

We invite you to be part of this new ministry. Please join us for a short presentation of the program and for questions and clarification. Our hope is that your participation in this meeting will give further direction to us and be of benefit to you as we work for the good of the people of our parish.

The meeting is planned for _____

from _____ to _____

in _____

Sincerely,

A Ministry of Consolation: Involving Your Parish in the Order of Christian Funerals

Dear

We are in the process of developing a ministry of consolation in our parish to assist our parishioners at the time of the death of a loved one. The thrust for such a program grows out of the revision of the *Order of Christian Funerals.*

The *Order of Christian Funerals* states: "Music is integral to the funeral rites. It allows the community to express convictions and feelings that words alone may fail to convey. It has the power to console and uplift the mourners and to strengthen the unity of the assembly in faith and love" (*OCF* #30). Not only are these strong words, they are sound words. They speak eloquently of the part you play in the process at the time of death.

We invite you to be part of this new ministry. Please join us for a short presentation of the program and for questions and clarification. Our hope is that your participation in this meeting will give further direction to us and be of benefit to you as we work for the good of the people of our parish.

The meeting is planned for _____

from _____ to _____

in _____

Sincerely,

A Ministry of Consolation

"Blessed are those that mourn . . ."

From the very words of Jesus in his Sermon on the Mount comes the latest ministry to the people of our parish by the people of our parish. Jesus taught that those who were mourning the loss of a loved one were to be seen as in need of the care and concern of his disciples, now the Christian community. A new impetus for this ancient ministry of the church is found in the *Order of Christian Funerals.*

> In the face of death, the Church confidently proclaims that God has created each person for eternal life and that Jesus, the Son of God, by his death and resurrection, has broken the chains of sin and death that bound humanity. Christ "achieved his task of redeeming humanity and giving perfect glory to God, principally by the paschal mystery of his blessed passion, resurrection from the dead, and glorious ascension" (*OCF* #1).

> The celebration of the Christian funeral brings hope and consolation to the living. While proclaiming the Gospel of Jesus Christ and witnessing the Christian hope in the resurrection, the funeral rites also recall to all who take part in them God's mercy and judgment and meet the human need to turn always to God in times of crisis (*OCF* #7).

Today, in its funeral rites, the Church asks that the entire community, priest and laity, be involved in ministering to the family of the deceased. All are called to pray with the family; some are called to specific ministries of service either in the leading of prayer or in providing the very atmosphere in which the prayer will take place.

The ministry of consolation consists of parishioners ministering to parishioners. This is the vision set forth by the church in this revision of the rites. The laity is called to a full, active ministry, one that will be both a source of strength and encouragement to the grieving and a fulfilling challenge to the one who ministers.

A Ministry of Consolation

"If one member suffers . . ."

I remember my grandfather's funeral Mass years ago. Black vestments worn by the priest, the absence of flowers, and somber chants set a stark mood that emphasized the sorrowful aspects of death, almost to the exclusion of any paschal motifs. The rite concentrated on themes of sin, guilt, and punishment, fear of the awesome God, and the need for intercession. They sang the *Dies Irae* as I followed the English in my missal with some horror. What did the "day of wrath" have to do with the gentle man who always had time and patience to spare for a grandchild?

My father died last March. All the same feelings were there: the pain, the questioning, the bewilderment, the sense of loneliness, the anger. These feelings were balanced, however, with those of hope through the proclamation of the Gospel—the Good News of the Resurrection. We recognized that the Resurrection comes at a price: the cross of suffering which eventually becomes the cross of glory.

His funeral Mass was a time for us to retell the story of Jesus and Our Savior's triumphant refusal to let death have the last word. We chose readings and prayers that spoke to our needs and memories. We sang songs and hymns that reflected our taste and spoke to our hearts. We wove our concerns into the General Intercessions. As we mourned, we also celebrated the hope Christ's death and Resurrection holds for us.

The balance we felt is a direct result of the changes in the funeral rite that came from the *Order of Christian Funerals*. The *Order* preserves the balance between praying for the dead and celebrating resurrection, acknowledges that funerals are for the living, and consoles the bereaved. It also calls all of us to help!

The challenge that the new rite offers has been accepted by our parish. Our Ministry of Consolation acknowledges that, "If one member suffers in the body of Christ which is the Church, all the members suffer with that member" (1 Corinthians 12:26). When death visits a family, a journey of separation begins and the Church is seen as a journey partner throughout the entire process. We console and comfort by offering hope in the name of the risen Jesus, helping to plan the funeral rites, and organizing whatever needs to be done, and we call on all in the parish to participate.

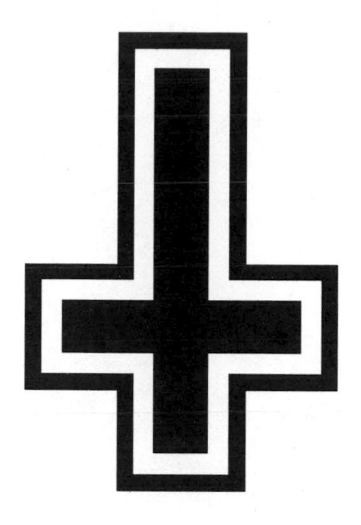

May the knowledge
that our thoughts
and prayers
are with you
at this time of sorrow
ease your heart
and give you strength.

Ministry of Consolation   Coordinator Information Form

Name of Deceased: _____

Date of Death:_____ Date of Funeral: _____

Nearest Kin/Relationship: _____

Address: _____

Phone: _____

Companion: _____

Cake Baker: _____

Booklet People: _____

Greeters: _____

Priest: _____

    Notified: _____ Altar Server: _____

    Wake Service: _____ Lector(s): _____

Sacristan Called: _____ EME: _____

Musician Called: _____

Follow-Up:

    First Anniversary Card (date sent) _____

    Second Month (Invitation to Prayer Service) _____

    Third Anniversary Card (date sent) _____

    Fourth Month (Invitation to Prayer Service) _____

    Fifth Month Card (date sent) _____

    Sixth Month (Invitation to Prayer Service) _____

    Invitation to All Souls Day Liturgy _____

Coordinator: _____

FAMILY INFORMATION

Deceased _____

Companion _____

1.   Names of relatives to be mentioned (include spouse, children, children's spouses, grandchildren, siblings, parents, stepchildren, etc.)

2.   How person died (sudden? long- or short-term illness? suicide? accident?)

3.   Faith life (very active in church? attended Mass? not practicing?)

4.   Person's occupation, hobbies, interests

5.   Family's description of person (e.g., "good husband," "loving mother," "very loyal and giving," etc.

6.   Other information (including special family situations)

Ministry of Consolation

Selection Sheet

NOTES

SELECTIONS

Name _____

Date _____

Celebrant _____

Placing of the Pall _____

_____

Entrance Song _____

Placing of Christian Symbols _____

First Reading _____

Read by _____

Responsorial Psalm _____

Second Reading _____

Read by _____

Gospel _____

General Intercessions:

Form _____

Prepared by Family _____

Read by _____

Gifts Brought Forward by _____

_____

_____

Song at Preparation of Gifts _____

Communion Song _____

Family Comments before Departure _____

Final Commendation Song _____

Recessional Song _____

Seating for First Few Rows _____

_____

Ministry of Consolation

Mass of Christian Burial

A Ministry of Consolation: Involving Your Parish in the Order of Christian Funerals

MASS OF CHRISTIAN BURIAL

Date

Name

Presider, _____
Altar Server, _____
Organist, _____
Vocalist, _____

Assisted by members of
the Ministry of Consolation

EUCHARIST PRAYER

We begin the eucharistic service of praise and thanksgiving, the center of the entire celebration, the central prayer of worship. At the priest's invitation we lift our hearts to God and unite with him in the words he addresses to the Father through Jesus Christ. Together we join Christ in his sacrifice, celebrating his memorial in the holy meal and acknowledging with him the wonderful works of God in our lives.

COMMUNION RITE

The Lord's Prayer

Sign of Peace

As a community of Christians joined by the Spirit in love, we express, deepen, and restore peaceful unity by the sign of peace.

COMMUNION PROCESSION   TITLE

FINAL COMMENDATION

INVITATION TO PRAYER

Our final farewell is an act of respect as we entrust _____ to the tender merciful embrace of God.

SILENT PRAYER

SIGNS OF FAREWELL

Incense is a sign of reverence and of farewell as our community's prayers for _____ rise to the throne of God.

SONG OF FAREWELL   TITLE

PRAYER OF COMMENDATION

Our community calls upon God's mercy, commends into his hands, and affirms our belief that those who have died in Christ will share in Christ's victory over death.

RECESSIONAL SONG   TITLE

INTRODUCTORY RITES

PASCHAL CANDLE

The Easter candle is a sign to us of Christ's undying presence, of his victory over sin and death, and of our share in that victory by virtue of our initiation.

HOLY WATER

The blessing with holy water reminds us of the saving waters of baptism—a proclamation of the death and life into which _____ entered through the waters of baptism. Our community acknowledges _____ as one of our own, as one who was welcomed in baptism and who held a place in our assembly.

PLACING OF THE PALL

The Funeral Pall is a reminder of the garment given at Baptism and a sign of the life in Christ lived by _____. It will be placed by _____.

ENTRANCE PROCESSION   TITLE

OPENING PRAYER

LITURGY OF THE WORD

The readings proclaim the paschal mystery, teach remembrance of the dead, convey the hope of being gathered together again in God's kingdom, and encourage the witness of Christian life. The readings tell of God's design for a world in which suffering and death will relinquish their hold on all whom God has called his own.

FIRST READING
read by

Reading
Explanation

RESPONSORIAL PSALM

SECOND READING
read by

Reading
Explanation

GOSPEL

HOMILY

GENERAL INTERCESSIONS

In union with the risen Lord, we pray for the living and the dead, confident that our prayer will be heard.

LITURGY OF THE EUCHARIST

PRESENTATION OF GIFTS

_____ will present the gifts of bread and wine, which will become for us the gift of Eucharist.

SONG AT THE PRESENTATION OF GIFTS   TITLE

PRAYER OVER THE GIFTS

Priest: *Pray, brethren, that our sacrifice may be acceptable to God, the almighty Father.*

People: May the Lord accept the sacrifice at your hands for the praise and glory of his name for our good, and the good of all his Church.

Priest: (*prayer*)

People: Amen.

*All who have recently
lost a loved one
are invited to a
Special Prayer Service
and Hospitality.*

In Remembrance

_____

_____

_____

_____

Prayer Services to Gather Families Together at a Future Date

The assembly gathers in an atmosphere of minimal lighting. At the appointed hour, one of the companions offers a brief welcome and introduction. At the end of this welcome, all are invited to stand. The presider, a companion carrying the Paschal candle (if possible), and a companion carrying the Book of Names of the Dead assemble in the rear of the church. The companion raises the Paschal candle and a Light Proclamation is sung.

After the Light Proclamation, all join in singing an opening song. During the opening song, the presider and two companions process to the sanctuary. The presider goes to his chair; the companions place the Paschal candle and Book of the Names of the Dead in their places and then go to their chairs.

[After the opening song, the presider greets the assembly.]

Presider: In the name of the Father, and of the Son, and of the Holy Spirit. Amen.
May the God of hope give you the fullness of peace,
and may the Lord of life be always with you.

All: And also with you.

[The presider briefly welcomes the people and then prays the opening prayer.]

Presider: Let us pray.
Father of mercies and God of all consolation,
you pursue us with untiring love
and dispel the shadow of death
with the bright dawn of life.

Comfort us in our loss and sorrow.
Be our refuge and our strength, O Lord,
and lift us from the depths of grief
into the peace and light of your presence.

Your Son our Lord Jesus Christ,
by dying, has destroyed our death,
and by rising, has restored our life.
Enable us therefore to press on toward him,
so that, after our earthly course is run,
he may reunite us with those we love,
when every tear will be wiped away.

We ask this through Christ our Lord. Amen.

[All are seated for the psalmody. Psalms 121, 27, and 91 may be sung or recited antiphonally.]

A reader then proclaims the reading, John 14:1-6.

After the reading, the presider delivers the homily.

After the homily, those who have lost loved ones are led forward by the companions to write the names of the deceased in the Book of Names of the Dead. While this procession and writing are taking place, "Blest Are They" or some other appropriate song is sung.

After the inscription of names, all stand for the intercessions. These intercessions may be taken from the Office of the Dead or be composed by the Ministry of Consolation. After the intercessions, the presider leads the Our Father.

Presider: With God there is mercy and fullness of redemption;
                let us pray as Jesus taught us:
                Our Father . . .

[After the Our Father, all remain standing as the presider prays the concluding prayer.]

Presider: God, our creator and redeemer,
                by your power Christ conquered death
                and returned to you in glory.
                May all your people who have gone before us in faith
                share his victory
                and enjoy the vision of your glory for ever,
                where Christ lives and reigns with you and the Holy Spirit,
                one God, for ever and ever. Amen.

Presider: The Lord be with you.

All: And also with you.

Presider: May the peace of God,
                which is beyond all understanding,
                keep your hearts and minds
                in the knowledge and love of God
                and of his Son, our Lord Jesus Christ.
                May almighty God bless you,
                the Father, and the Son, and the Holy Spirit.

[All then join in singing the closing song.]

Ministry of Consolation

Prayer Service

Stand

OPENING SONG

OPENING PRAYER

Sit

PSALM 27

Presider: The Lord is my light and my salvation.

All: The Lord is my light and my salvation.

Side 1: The Lord is my light and my salvation;
whom should I fear?
The Lord is my life's refuge;
of whom should I be afraid?

Side 2: One thing I ask of the Lord;
this I seek:
to dwell in the house of the Lord
all the days of my life,
That I may gaze on the loveliness of the Lord
and contemplate his temple.

Side 1: Hear, O Lord, the sound of my call;
have pity on me, and answer me.
Your presence, O Lord, I seek.
Hide not your face from me.

Side 2: I believe that I shall see the bounty of the Lord
in the land of the living.
Wait for the Lord with courage;
be stouthearted, and wait for the Lord.

Side 1: Glory to the Father, and to the Son,
and to the Holy Spirit.

Side 2: As it was in the beginning, is now, and
ever shall be,
world without end. Amen.

All: The Lord is my light and my salvation.

PSALM 91

Stand

PRAYER

GOSPEL   *John 14:1-6*

HOMILY

Those who have lost a loved one are led forward by the companions to write the names of the deceased in the Book of Names of the Dead.

PROCESSIONAL SONG

Stand

INTERCESSIONS

Response: Lord, you are our life and resurrection.

OUR FATHER

CLOSING SONG

Ministry of Consolation

General Intercessions

DIRECTIONS FOR PRINTING THE
GENERAL INTERCESSIONS BOOKLET

This booklet is set up to be copied back-to-back as it is printed in this book, then collated in page order and folded in the middle. It also can be stapled on the fold.

The first sheet (the front and back covers on this page) is copied back-to-back with the second sheet (pages 2 and 23); the third sheet (pages 3 and 22) is copied back-to-back with the fourth (pages 4 and 21); and so on.

To accomplish this on a machine that copies back-to-back automatically, the book can just be moved across the copy machine; there is no need to flip it back and forth or upside down. The booklet will be collated and ready to fold as it is printed.

Suggestions

For _____ who preceded _____ in death, that they be united in the eternal kingdom of peace.

Confident in the knowledge that _____ is now at peace, that time softens our pain until all that remains is the beauty of our memories of _____ and the love, always the love that he/she shared so generously.

That the many families of the world grow closer together in a celebration of their different gifts so that they may find comfort in the presence and truth of your care.

General Intercessions

Having heard the word of God proclaimed and preached, the assembly responds . . . with prayers of intercession for the deceased and all the dead, for the family and all who mourn, and for all in the assembly. The holy people of God, confident in their belief in the communion of saints, exercise their royal priesthood by joining together in this prayer for all those who have died (OCF #29).

Several models of intercessions are provided. You may use one of the following forms, combine parts of several together, adapt parts, or compose your own. Additional suggestions are on the last page.

To invite the people's response, an invitation at the end of each petition needs to be added like:

"Lord, in your mercy,"
"Let us pray to the Lord,"
or
"To you we pray."

3

General Intercessions   Form 1

Priest begins:

Brothers and sisters, Jesus Christ is risen from the dead and sits at the right hand of the Father, where he intercedes for his Church. Confident that God hears the voice of those who trust in the Lord Jesus, we join our prayers to his:

_____

(hold out arm)   Response: _____ .

Reader says:

The response is "Hear our prayer."
(hold out arm as a motion for people to answer)

In baptism _____ received the light of Christ. Scatter the darkness now and lead him/her over the waters of death.
Lord, in your mercy:

_____

(hold out arm)   Response: _____ .

(hold out arm)   Response: *Hear our prayer.*

Our brother/sister _____ was nourished at the table of the Savior. Welcome him/her into the halls of the heavenly banquet.
Lord, in your mercy:

_____

(hold out arm)   Response: *Hear our prayer.*

Many friends and members of our families have gone before us and await the kingdom. Grant them an everlasting home with your Son.
Lord, in your mercy:

_____

(hold out arm)   Response: _____ .

(hold out arm)   Response: *Hear our prayer.*

General Intercessions

Form 9
A deceased child

Priest begins:

Reader says:

The response is _____ .
(hold out arm as a motion for people to answer)

_____

_____

_____

(hold out arm) Response: _____

_____

_____

_____

(hold out arm) Response: _____

Many people die by violence, war, and famine each day. Show your mercy to those who suffer so unjustly these sins against your love, and gather them to the eternal kingdom of peace. Lord, in your mercy:
(hold out arm) Response: Hear our prayer.

Those who trusted in the Lord now sleep in the Lord. Give refreshment, rest, and peace to all whose faith is known to you alone. Lord, in your mercy:
(hold out arm) Response: Hear our prayer.

The family and friends of _____ seek comfort and consolation. Heal their pain and dispel the darkness and doubt that come from grief. Lord, in your mercy:
(hold out arm) Response: Hear our prayer.

We are assembled here in faith and confidence to pray for our brother/sister _____ . Strengthen our hope so that we may live in the expectation of your Son's coming. Lord, in your mercy:
(hold out arm) Response: Hear our prayer.

Priest concludes:

Lord God,
giver of peace and healer of souls,
hear the prayers of the Redeemer, Jesus Christ,
and the voices of your people,
whose lives were purchased by the blood of the Lamb.
Forgive the sins of all who sleep in Christ
and grant them a place in the kingdom.

We ask this through Christ our Lord.
We respond: Amen.

General Intercessions   Form 2

Priest begins:

God, the almighty Father, raised Christ his Son from the dead; with confidence we ask him to save all his people, living and dead.

Reader says:

The response is "Lord, hear our prayer."
(hold out arm as a motion for people to answer)

For _____ who in baptism was given the pledge of eternal life, that he/she may now be admitted to the company of the saints.
We pray to the Lord.
(hold out arm)   *Response: Lord, hear our prayer.*

For our brother/sister who ate the body of Christ, the bread of life, that he/she may be raised up on the last day.
We pray to the Lord.
(hold out arm)   *Response: Lord, hear our prayer.*

For the family and friends of our brother/sister _____, that they may be consoled in their grief by the Lord, who wept at the death of his friend Lazarus.
We pray to the Lord.
(hold out arm)   *Response: Lord, hear our prayer.*

For all parents who grieve over the death of their children, that they may be comforted in the knowledge that their children dwell with God.
We pray to the Lord.
(hold out arm)   *Response: Lord, hear our prayer.*

For children who have died of hunger and disease, that these little ones be seated close to the Lord at his heavenly table.
We pray to the Lord.
(hold out arm)   *Response: Lord, hear our prayer.*

For the whole Church, that we may prepare worthily for the hour of our death, when God will call us by name to pass from this world to the next.
We pray to the Lord.
(hold out arm)   *Response: Lord, hear our prayer.*

Priest concludes:

Lord God,
you entrusted _____ to our care
and now you embrace him/her in your love.

Take _____ into your keeping
together with all children who have died.

Comfort us, your sorrowing servants,
who seek to do your will
and to know your saving peace.
We ask this through Christ our Lord.
We respond: Amen.

General Intercessions   Form 8
A deceased child

Priest begins:

Let us pray for _____, his/her family and friends, and for all God's people.

Reader says:

The response is "Lord, hear our prayer."
(hold out arm as a motion for people to answer)

For _____, child of God [and heir to the kingdom], that he/she be held securely in God's loving embrace now and for eternity.
We pray to the Lord.
(hold out arm)   *Response: Lord, hear our prayer.*

For _____'s family, especially his/her mother and father, [his/her brother(s) and sister(s),] that they feel the healing power of Christ in the midst of their pain and grief.
We pray to the Lord.
(hold out arm)   *Response: Lord, hear our prayer.*

For _____'s friends, those who played with him/her and those who cared for him/her, that they may be consoled in their loss and strengthened in their love for one another.
We pray to the Lord.
(hold out arm)   *Response: Lord, hear our prayer.*

For our deceased relatives and friends and for all who have helped us, that they may have the reward of their goodness.
We pray to the Lord.
(hold out arm)   *Response: Lord, hear our prayer.*

For those who have fallen asleep in the hope of rising again, that they may see God face to face.
We pray to the Lord.
(hold out arm)   *Response: Lord, hear our prayer.*

For all of us assembled here to worship in faith, that we may be gathered together again in God's kingdom.
We pray to the Lord.
(hold out arm)   *Response: Lord, hear our prayer.*

For _____

_____
We pray to the Lord.
(hold out arm)   *Response: Lord, hear our prayer.*

Priest concludes:

God, our shelter and our strength,
you listen in love to the cry of your people:
hear the prayers we offer for our departed brothers and sisters.
Cleanse them of their sins
and grant them the fullness of redemption.
We ask this through Christ our Lord.

We respond: Amen.

General Intercessions

Form 3

Priest begins:

My dear friends, let us join with one another in praying to God, not only for our departed brother/sister, but also for the Church, for peace in the world, and for ourselves.

Reader says:

The response is "Lord, hear our prayer."
(hold out arm as a motion for people to answer)

That the bishops and priests of the Church, and all who preach the Gospel, may be given the strength to express in action the word they proclaim.
We pray to the Lord.
(hold out arm)   Response: Lord, hear our prayer.

That those in public office may promote justice and peace.
We pray to the Lord.
(hold out arm)   Response: Lord, hear our prayer.

That those who bear the cross of pain in mind or body may never feel forsaken by God.
We pray to the Lord.
(hold out arm)   Response: Lord, hear our prayer.

That God may deliver the soul of his servant _____ from punishment and from the powers of darkness.
We pray to the Lord.
(hold out arm)   Response: Lord, hear our prayer.

You took upon yourself the suffering and death of us all.
To you we pray:
(hold out arm)   Response: Bless us and keep us, O Lord.

You promised to raise up those who believe in you just as you were raised up in glory by the Father.
To you we pray:
(hold out arm)   Response: Bless us and keep us, O Lord.

To you we pray:
(hold out arm)   Response: Bless us and keep us, O Lord.

Priest concludes:

Lord God,
you entrusted _____ to our care
and now you embrace him/her in your love.
Take _____ into your keeping
together with all children who have died.
Comfort us, your sorrowing servants,
who seek to do your will
and to know your saving peace.
We ask this through Christ our Lord.
We respond: Amen.

General Intercessions   Form 7

A baptized child

Priest begins:

The Lord Jesus is the lover of his people and our only sure hope. Let us ask him to deepen our faith and sustain us in this dark hour.

Reader says:

The response is "Bless us and keep us, O Lord."
(hold out arm as a motion for people to answer)

You became a little child for our sake, sharing our human life.
To you we pray:
(hold out arm)   *Response: Bless us and keep us, O Lord.*

You grew in wisdom, age, and grace, and learned obedience through suffering.
To you we pray:
(hold out arm)   *Response: Bless us and keep us, O Lord.*

You welcomed children, promising them your kingdom.
To you we pray:
(hold out arm)   *Response: Bless us and keep us, O Lord.*

You comforted those who mourned the loss of children and friends.
To you we pray:
(hold out arm)   *Response: Bless us and keep us, O Lord.*

That God in his mercy may blot out all his/her offenses.
We pray to the Lord.
(hold out arm)   *Response: Lord, hear our prayer.*

That God may establish him/her in light and peace.
We pray to the Lord.
(hold out arm)   *Response: Lord, hear our prayer.*

That God may call him/her to happiness in the company of all the saints.
We pray to the Lord.
(hold out arm)   *Response: Lord, hear our prayer.*

That God may welcome into his glory those of our family and friends who have departed this life.
We pray to the Lord.
(hold out arm)   *Response: Lord, hear our prayer.*

That God may give a place in the kingdom of heaven to all the faithful departed.
We pray to the Lord.
(hold out arm)   *Response: Lord, hear our prayer.*

Priest concludes:

O God,
Creator and Redeemer of all the faithful,
grant to the souls of your departed servants
release from all their sins.
Hear our prayers for those we love
and give them the pardon they have always desired.
We ask this through Christ our Lord.

We respond: Amen.

General Intercessions   Form 4

Priest begins:

Brothers and sisters, Jesus Christ is risen from the dead and sits at the right hand of the Father where he intercedes for his Church. Confident that God hears the voices of those who trust in the Lord Jesus, we join our prayers to his:

Reader says:

The response is "Hear our prayer."
(hold out arm as a motion for people to answer)

In baptism _____ received the light of Christ. Scatter the darkness now and lead him/her over the waters of death. Lord, in you mercy.
(hold out arm)   *Response: Hear our prayer.*

Our brother/sister _____ was nourished at the table of the Savior. Welcome him/her into the halls of the heavenly banquet. Lord, in your mercy:
(hold out arm)   *Response: Hear our prayer.*

Many friends and members of our families have gone before us and await the kingdom. Grant them an everlasting home with your Son. Lord, in your mercy.
(hold out arm)   *Response: Hear our prayer.*

That God will grant release to those who suffer. Let us pray to the Lord.
(hold out arm)   *Response: Lord, have mercy.*

That God will grant peace to all who have died in the faith of Christ. Let us pray to the Lord.
(hold out arm)   *Response: Lord, have mercy.*

That one day we may all share in the banquet of the Lord, praising God for victory over death. Let us pray to the Lord.
(hold out arm)   *Response: Lord, have mercy.*

Priest concludes:

Lord God, you entrusted _____ to our care and now you embrace him/her in your love. Comfort us, your sorrowing servants, who seek to do your will and to know your saving peace. We ask this through Christ our Lord.

We respond: Amen.

Many people die by violence, war, and famine each day. Show your mercy to those who suffer so unjustly these sins against your love, and gather them to the eternal kingdom of peace.

Lord, in your mercy.
(hold out arm)   Response: Hear our prayer.

Those who trusted in the Lord now sleep in the Lord. Give refreshment, rest, and peace to all whose faith is known to you alone.

Lord, in your mercy.
(hold out arm)   Response: Hear our prayer.

The family and friends of _____ seek comfort and consolation. Heal their pain and dispel the darkness and doubt that come from grief.

Lord, in your mercy.
(hold out arm)   Response: Hear our prayer.

We are assembled here in faith and confidence to pray for our brother/sister _____. Strengthen our hope so that we may live in the expectation of your Son's coming.

Lord, in your mercy.
(hold out arm)   Response: Hear our prayer.

Priest concludes:

Lord God,
giver of peace and healer of souls,
hear the prayers of the Redeemer, Jesus Christ,
and the voices of your people,
whose lives were purchased by the blood of the Lamb.
Forgive the sins of all who sleep in Christ
and grant them a place in the kingdom.

We ask this through Christ our Lord.

We respond: Amen.

General Intercessions   *Form 6*
A baptized child

Priest begins:

Jesus is the Son of God and the pattern for our own creation. His promise is that one day we shall truly be like him. With our hope founded on that promise, we pray:

Reader says:

The response is "Lord, have mercy."
(hold out arm as a motion for people to answer)

That God will receive our praise and thanksgiving for the life of _____.
Let us pray to the Lord.
(hold out arm)   Response: Lord, have mercy.

That God will bring to completion _____'s baptism into Christ.
Let us pray to the Lord.
(hold out arm)   Response: Lord, have mercy.

That God will lead _____ from death to life.
Let us pray to the Lord.
(hold out arm)   Response: Lord, have mercy.

That all of us, _____'s family and friends, may be comforted in our grief.
Let us pray to the Lord.
(hold out arm)   Response: Lord, have mercy.

Priest begins:

Let us turn to Christ Jesus with confidence and faith in the power of his cross and resurrection:

Reader says:

The response is "Lord have mercy."
(hold out arm as a motion for people to answer)

Risen Lord, pattern of our life for ever:
Lord, have mercy.
(hold out arm)   Response: *Lord, have mercy.*

Promise and image of what we shall be:
Lord, have mercy.
(hold out arm)   Response: *Lord, have mercy.*

Son of God who came to destroy sin and death:
Lord, have mercy.
(hold out arm)   Response: *Lord, have mercy.*

Word of God who delivered us from fear of death:
Lord, have mercy.
(hold out arm)   Response: *Lord, have mercy.*

Crucified Lord, forsaken in death, raised in glory:
Lord, have mercy.
(hold out arm)   Response: *Lord, have mercy.*

Lord Jesus, gentle Shepherd who brings rest to our souls, give peace to _____ for ever.
Lord, have mercy.
(hold out arm)   Response: *Lord, have mercy.*

Lord Jesus, you bless those who mourn and are in pain.
Bless _____'s family and friends who gather around him/her today:
Lord, have mercy.
(hold out arm)   Response: *Lord, have mercy.*

_____

Lord, in your mercy:
(hold out arm)   Response: *Lord, have mercy.*

Priest concludes:

Lord God,
you entrusted _____ to our care
and now you embrace him/her in your love.
Comfort us, your sorrowing servants,
who seek to do your will
and to know your saving peace.
We ask this through Christ our Lord.
We respond: Amen.